Entrepreneur's Toolkit

Harvard Business Essentials

The New Manager's Guide and Mentor

The Harvard Business Essentials series is designed to provide comprehensive advice, personal coaching, background information, and guidance on the most relevant topics in business. Drawing on rich content from Harvard Business School Publishing and other sources, these concise guides are carefully crafted to provide a highly practical resource for readers with all levels of experience, and will prove especially valuable for the new manager. To ensure quality and accuracy, each volume is closely reviewed by a specialized content adviser from a world-class business school. Whether you are a new manager seeking to expand your skills or a seasoned professional looking to broaden your knowledge base, these solution-oriented books put reliable answers at your fingertips.

Entrepreneur's Toolkit

Tools and Techniques to Launch and
Grow Your New Business

Harvard Business School Press | *Boston, Massachusetts*

978-1-59139-436-5 (ISBN 13)
Library of Congress Cataloging-in-Publication Data
Harvard business essentials: entrepreneur's toolkit : tools and techniques to launch and grow your new business.
p. cm.—(The Harvard business essentials series)
Includes bibliographical references and index.
ISBN 1-59139-436-8
1. New business enterprises. I. Harvard Business School. II. Series.
HD62.5.H37378 2004
658.1'1—dc22
2004010859

Contents

Entrepreneur's Toolkit

Introduction

"I seen my opportunities and I took 'em." That is how George Washington Plunkitt, a member of New York City's corrupt Tammany Hall political machine, summarized his lucrative career of "honest graft." Plunkitt was a scoundrel and a crook, and yet his pithy statement provides us with a good working definition of an *entrepreneur*: a person who identifies an opportunity and pursues it. A century later, William Bygrave, a scholar and practitioner of the entrepreneurial arts, extended this definition, describing an entrepreneur as someone who not only perceives an opportunity but also "creates an organization to pursue it."[1]

That last part of Bygrave's definition is essential. Opportunities as we generally understand them are most effectively addressed through organizations formed by entrepreneurs. Thomas Edison, for example, recognized the business opportunity in urban electric illumination. Most people know that he pursued it through tireless laboratory experiments that eventually produced a workable incandescent light bulb. But invention was only part of Edison's genius. He also formed a company in which he brought together the human and financial resources needed to implement his vision of commercial and residential lighting. That company was the forerunner of the General Electric Company, one of today's largest and most powerful enterprises.

We observe the same formula repeatedly: recognizing opportunity and addressing it through an organization. For example, in 1983, Howard Schultz, manager of retail operations for a small Seattle coffee vendor called Starbucks, recognized such an opportunity while vacationing in Europe. He was impressed by the popularity of espresso bistros of Milan and believed that Americans would appreciate a similar café ambiance and a high-quality product. Upon returning, Schultz convinced his employer to test the espresso bar concept on its home turf. The success of the Seattle experiment encouraged Schultz to form his own organization, Il Giornale, in 1985. Within two years, Il Giornale acquired Starbucks, adopted its name, and, with the capital of private investors, began its pursuit of coffee aficionados. By 2003, Starbucks had more than 7,200 retail outlets and reported revenues in excess of $4 billion.

A complete definition of the entrepreneur must also recognize one other factor: risk. In the financial world, risk contains the possibility of both gain and loss. The entrepreneur puts "skin in the game"—usually in the form of time and personal savings. If the venture goes badly, his or her time and hard-earned savings are lost. But if things go well, the entrepreneur can reap a sizable profit.

Economic history is filled with stories like those of Edison and Schultz. One is the story of Dan Bricklin, inventor of the now ubiquitous electronic spreadsheet (VisiCalc) and founder of Software Arts, Inc. Rollin King and Herb Kelleher saw an opportunity in short-haul, low-cost air travel and turned that concept into Southwest Airlines, the most profitable U.S. air carrier. And, of course, Bill Gates was the young programming geek who grabbed onto the coattails of the burgeoning microcomputing phenomenon and rode them to a huge bonanza.

For every entrepreneur recounted in the history books and the popular press, thousands of others go unrecognized because they are either small or serve a limited geographical area: a chain of ten car wash facilities; a five-employee company that installs and repairs home office and small-business computer systems; a married couple that owns and operates two small restaurants and a catering service. These unsung entrepreneurs are fundamentally no different from their more glorified counterparts. At bottom, all of them do the same thing. They recognize a commercial opportunity and pursue it through an organization, their own managerial or technical talents, and some combination of human and financial capital, as described in figure I-1. And they bear the risks of success or failure. In a nut-shell, that is what Thomas Edison did. It is what Howard Schultz and Bill Gates did—and it is what every enterprising business owner in your community has done. And you will have to do the same if you aspire to be a successful entrepreneur.

Some scholars differentiate entrepreneurial firms from what they call *lifestyle enterprises*. A lifestyle enterprise is a business venture with modest revenue and growth expectations. The owner is simply look-ing for a venture that will satisfy the financial needs of his or her fam-ily. It might be a retail store, a law firm, a chicken farm, or a shop that fixes home appliances. There is no expectation of creating a national franchise of the business or of selling it after five years to one of the *Fortune* 500 companies for a huge windfall. No venture capitalists will come calling. One author, William E. Wetzel Jr., has described lifestyle enterprises as ventures with five-year revenue projections of less than $10 million. In his opinion, more than 90 percent of all start-ups are lifestyle ventures.[2]

But even with small expectations, the founder of a lifestyle busi-ness nevertheless fits our definition of an entrepreneur in that the

FIGURE I-1

The Entrepreneurial Process

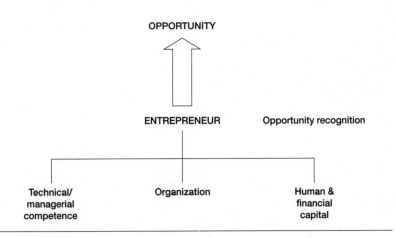

founder identifies an opportunity, creates an organization and marshals resources to pursue it, and bears the risk. Thus, the lifestyle entrepreneur will find applications for most of the materials covered in this book.

The Role of Entrepreneurs

Entrepreneurs play an important role in every free-market society. As described by economist Joseph Schumpeter in the 1930s, entrepreneurs act as a force for creative destruction, sweeping away established technologies, products, and ways of doing things and replacing them with others that the marketplace as a whole sees as representing greater value. In this sense entrepreneurs are agents of change and, hopefully, progress. Thus, entrepreneurs displaced home kerosene lamps with brighter and cleaner-burning gas in the mid- to late 1800s. Those gas lamps, in turn, were displaced by Edison's incandescent electric light system, which provided better performance and greater safety. Fluorescent lighting came along years later, displacing many incandescent applications.

We see this pattern repeated in virtually every industry. Entrepreneurs invent or commercialize new technologies that displace the old. Photocopying, the personal computer, and new and improved drug therapies are all products of enterprising entrepreneurs. Entrepreneurs also introduce products and services that deliver something entirely new: the electronic calculator, next-day package delivery, the World Wide Web, aircraft simulation software, oral contraceptives, angioplasty to open narrow heart arteries, and laser surgery to bring eyesight to near 20/20.

Entrepreneurs have given us even mundanely useful things that our parents or grandparents would not have imagined: personal digital assistants (à la the Palm Pilot), contact lenses, one-hour photo processing, milk in aseptic packaging that requires no refrigeration, online auctions that bring together buyers and sellers from every part of the world, and on and on.

It is important to acknowledge that entrepreneurs do more than just think of new concepts and recognize their commercial opportunities. They take the next step: forming enterprises and marshaling resources to address them. This step separates the entrepreneur from the inventor and delivers value and choice to society. This step is almost always risky because success in not preordained.

Entrepreneurs generally make positive contributions to society. They find and exploit opportunities to provide goods and services that were previously unavailable or in limited supply. Henry Ford's early enterprise, for example, brought the automobile, once a plaything for the wealthy, within reach of the typical household. Entrepreneurs also find and exploit ways of providing higher-quality goods and services at lower prices. These contributions make free-market societies wealthy and dynamic, and, for most people, they make life much more interesting. They sweep away stagnant industries and replace them with growing ones that generate new employment opportunities, often at much higher wages.

Anyone who doubts the benefits of entrepreneurial contributions, should compare the experiences of the United States and the former Soviet Union in the post-World War II period. Those two nations had populations of roughly equal size. Both had strong central governments, substantial natural resources, and high levels of literacy and technical know-how. Yet in the fifty-year period following the war, the United States outpaced its rival on almost every front: food production, manufacturing, military might, housing, technical advancements, general health and longevity, per capita income, and the availability, quality, and variety of goods and services. In large measure, the Soviet Union's failures can be attributed to its centrally planned economy and its hostility to private property, both of which suppressed incentives to invent and to pursue commercial opportunities. In contrast, the American economy was unplanned. Its culture honored and supported entrepreneurs. Its laws safeguarded property, including intellectual property, and took some of the sting out of failure through bankruptcy provisions. Its unrestricted flows of capital allowed funds to move to enterprises with the most attractive risk/reward characteristics. While the Soviets suppressed the energy and acquisitiveness of individuals who had new ideas, the American system encouraged and glorified them. In the end, many of the economic failures of the Soviet Union and the successes of its rival can be attributed to their different treatment of entrepreneurs.

What's Ahead

This book takes a linear approach to the topics that concern entrepreneurs, from the initial question ("Am I the type of person who should start a business?") to the last issue that a successful business owner needs to consider ("How can I cash out of the business I've built?"). That linear approach may not correspond to the facts of life for every entrepreneurial venture, but it is a practical way to organize this book.

Chapter 1 describes the self-diagnosis that every prospective entrepreneur should undertake. Are you the right type of person to start up and operate a business? This chapter will help you answer that important question.

The first steps in the entrepreneurial process are to identify and evaluate business opportunities. Chapter 2 offers five characteristics you should look for in a business opportunity, the situations in which you are most likely to find them, and a process for evaluating their potential.

Assuming that you've found a powerful opportunity and are determined to pursue it, you must answer this question: "Should my business be a sole proprietorship, a partnership, a corporation, or something else?" Chapter 3 explains the various legal forms of business organization used in the United States, assesses their pros and cons, and explains how you can determine which is best for your venture.

Business model and *business strategy* are two terms that are tossed around freely, often without precision. What is a business model?

What is a business strategy? Chapter 4 uses two powerful examples to describe how the business model explains the way key components of the enterprise work together to make money. It also shows how strategy must be designed to differentiate the entity and confer it with a competitive advantage. Finally, it offers a five-step process for formulating strategy and aligning business activities with it.

Chapter 5 gets you started on writing a plan for your business. A business plan explains the opportunity, identifies the market to be served, and provides details about how the entrepreneurial organization plans to pursue it. It also describes the unique qualifications that the management team brings to the effort, lists the resources required for success, and provides a forecast of results over a reasonable time horizon. This chapter tells you why a business plan is necessary, gives you a format for organizing one, and offers tips for developing each section in the format. It also directs you to the Harvard Business Essentials series Web site, www.elearning.hbsp.org/businesstools. That site features a free, downloadable spreadsheet template you can use to develop pro forma financial statements for your business plan. While you're at the site, check out the other download materials— templates, checklists, and other tools—associated with other books in the series.

Chapter 6 concentrates on the financing requirements that businesses typically encounter in the various phases of their life cycles, from start-up to maturity. It also provides an overview of the sources you can turn to in securing financing during these phases. Two types of business—lifestyle and entrepreneurial—are used to illustrate the general course of financing from start-up through expansion.

To continue the discussion of financing, Chapter 7 addresses the fact that growing firms must obtain external capital. Entrepreneurs can bootstrap early development from personal sources, friends, and relatives, but external infusions of capital are usually necessary if they want to move to a higher level. This chapter introduces two sources of capital: business angels and venture capitalists. It describes these individuals, explains what attracts them, and discusses how you can connect with them.

At some point, growing firms with exceptional revenue potential seek and obtain financing through an initial public offering (IPO) of their shares to individual investors and institutional investors such as pension funds and mutual funds. That rare event results in a significant exchange of paper ownership shares for the hard cash the firm needs for stability and expansion. Chapter 8 describes what it takes to be an IPO candidate, the pros and cons of going public, the role of investment bankers, and eight steps for doing a deal. Because only an extremely small percentage of businesses will obtain external capital from an IPO, we also present an alternative arrangement: the private placement.

Chapter 9 is about the managerial challenge of enterprise growth. Entrepreneurs seek growth, often without thinking about how they will handle it, how they will keep it going, or whether they are up to the job. This chapter addresses the challenges of growth, with emphasis on how the role of the entrepreneur must change as the business expands. It highlights three key issues in sustaining growth, defines the various modes of management triggered by growth, and outlines options for changing the guard as the company becomes larger and more complex.

Paradoxically, success is sometimes the entrepreneurial company's greatest enemy; hierarchy, bureaucracy, and complacency are success's frequent companions. The danger of losing the entrepreneurial spirit and the ability to innovate should be a concern of every successful business founder. Chapter 10 explains why many companies lose their spark as they succeed and grow larger, and it suggests seven things that leaders can do to prevent it.

Chapter 11 is about harvesting your investment in a private business. Founders—and particularly the business angels and venture capitalists who support them—look forward to the day when they can turn their paper ownership into real money. This chapter describes the motivations that lead to harvesting, the primary mechanisms for doing so, and the methods used to answer the all-important question, "What is this business worth?"

Aids for the Entrepreneur

The back of this book contains material you may find very useful. The first is a series of appendixes. Appendix A is a primer on financial statements. If you haven't studied accounting or haven't thought about it for a long time, this will bring you up to speed. Appendix B explains details of breakeven analysis not covered in the book. Appendix C provides an overview of the methods used to determine the value of business enterprises. It won't make you a master of that very technical and specialized subject, but it will teach you enough that you can deal intelligently with valuation experts.

The next appendix, D, is a list of online sites you might want to surf to in gathering information about the ins and outs of business start-up and ownership. Finally, appendix E is taken directly from the U.S. Securities and Exchange Commission site. It explains Rule 144 on the sale of restricted and control stock. Few readers will ever need to understand Rule 144, but those who do may find this useful reading.

The appendixes are followed by a glossary of terms. Whenever you see an italicized term, that's your tip that its definition is contained in the glossary.

Next is a section titled "For Further Reading." There you'll find annotated references to recent books and articles—many of them classics—that provide much more material or unique insights into the topics covered in these chapters. If you'd like to learn more about any of the material we've included in the book, these references will help you.

Good luck with your entrepreneurial venture.

1

Self-Diagnosis

Do You Have the Right Stuff to Start a Business?

Key Topics Covered in This Chapter

- *tests for measuring an affinity for entrepreneurial work*

- *characteristics of successful entrepreneurs*

- *the effect of family background*

F EW ENTREPRENEURS INVENT things that change the way millions of people live or work. Dan Bricklin is an exception. In 1979, he and Bob Frankston created the first killer app of the personal computer age: an electronic spreadsheet they called VisiCalc. They formed a company to perfect and market this software, which, along with word processing programs, did more than almost anything else to fuel the growth of the personal computer industry.

As if to demonstrate that even a great invention is no assurance of commercial success, Bricklin's company, Software Arts, went belly-up. Its assets had to be sold to Lotus Development to avoid bankruptcy. But like many entrepreneurs, Bricklin went on to start other ventures. He became a serial entrepreneur, participating in four start-ups.

What is unique about people like Bricklin? What makes them tick? What are the personal traits and backgrounds of people who become successful entrepreneurs? This chapter addresses those questions and helps you determine whether you have the right stuff to be a business entrepreneur.

The Makings of an Entrepreneur

Many books and Web sites provide self-scoring tests that people can use to assess their fitness for entrepreneurial life. Here are some of the usual questions:

Can you tolerate a high level of risk?

Are you an overachiever?

Are you willing to put in ten- to twelve-hour days over an extended period, including weekends, to reach your goals?

Are you a self-starter?

Would you describe yourself as a good decision maker?

Are you willing to put your personal funds at risk?

Do you have the commitment required to build a business in the face of long hours and modest odds of success?

Such questions help people think through the personal side of entrepreneurial work and their fitness for it. This thought process is especially important for the would-be business owner who says, "I have a great idea for a business." Ideas are important, but rarely are they as important as personal background, motivation, and attitude. So take one or two of these self-tests and use the results to think deeply about your suitability for starting and operating an enterprise. (The U.S. Small Business Administration provides one on its site, www.sba.gov.)

Take these tests, but don't rely exclusively on their results because few of them are empirically based. Also, individual differences cannot be captured in a test. As scholar and practitioner William Bygrave has written, "Today, after more research, we know that there is no neat set of behavioral attributes that allow us to separate entrepreneurs from nonentrepreneurs."[1]

One of the few thorough studies on entrepreneurial characteristics was conducted between 1987 and 2002 by Walter Kuemmerle, an associate professor at Harvard Business School, who examined more than fifty start-up enterprises in twenty countries and across all industries. Some were successful; others were not. From this mixed bag Kuemmerle distilled five characteristics of successful entrepreneurs, a list he views as a litmus test for people who want to start their own businesses. He found that those characteristics are firm across industries and countries. Successful entrepreneurs, according to Kuemmerle,

1. are comfortable stretching the rules

2. are prepared to make powerful enemies

3. have the patience to start small

4. are willing to change strategy quickly

5. know how to close a deal[2]

Let's consider each of these characteristics in some detail.

Comfortable Stretching the Rules

Successful entrepreneurs are willing to bend the rules to get what they need: capital, able employees, contracts, or whatever it takes to achieve their ends. In a *Harvard Business Review* article on this subject Kuemmerle cites the example of a two-person direct-marketing start-up that, with venture capital money in hand, desperately needed to hire two dozen experienced marketers—and quickly. But what top-notch people would leave their jobs to join a company that didn't even have an office (the two principals were still working out of their homes)? To get over this problem, the entrepreneurs placed a sizable ad in a major business paper that described their little outfit as a "fast growing multinational company." Then they rented a plush office suite at a fashionable Four Seasons hotel for the day as an interviewing site. Per Kuemmerle, more than one thousand people responded. These owners got what they wanted by stretching the rules—and the truth.

Prepared to Make Powerful Enemies

It's always smart to pursue opportunities that will not put you in competition with a powerful rival—a big, entrenched company that has many resources. But this is not always possible. Entrepreneurs will not seek out a David and Goliath situation, but neither will they shrink from it. Michael Dell, for example, went up against IBM and other big personal computer makers when he began his fledgling company. But he did so with a twist: direct-to-consumer sales. Sam Walton did the same thing when he opened the first Wal-Mart store in Rogers, Arkansas, in 1962. He faced formidable competition from Sears, Kmart, and other mass-market merchandisers. So he challenged them indirectly, by locating his stores in small, rural communities that were unserved by the mega-retailers. Forty-two years later, the company Walton founded led the list of *Fortune* 500 companies, with revenues of $259 billion.

Have the Patience to Start Small

Most new ventures, no matter how well planned, are experiments. Starting small gives company founders an opportunity to test and fine-tune a commercial concept before they roll it out in a major way—that is, before they lock themselves into a business formula. Starting small gives them a chance to sense how customers respond to a product, its price, and the way it is served.

Perhaps the most spectacular and financially catastrophic start-up failure of the past ten years resulted from a start-up company whose leaders were unwilling to start small. This case involved Webvan, whose founders—including Louis Borders, founder of Borders Group—envisioned a nationwide system of grocery home-delivery. Webvan began by building a monster 330,000-square-foot automated warehouse in Oakland, California. It then raised more than $850 million in equity capital and began work on twenty-six similar facilities in metropolitan areas across the United States. But the company never came close to breaking even. Within two years it had burned through its cash and was forced into bankruptcy. By most estimates, Webvan had tried to do too much too fast.

By 2002, Louis Borders was back with a new venture, KeepMedia, which allowed Internet users to download articles from hundreds of periodicals on a pay-for-use basis. But he seemed to have learned the lesson of starting small. His new venture was more modest—with thirty-two employees versus the five thousand on the rolls of Webvan—and aimed to grow more slowly.

Willing to Shift Strategies Quickly

The future never unfolds as we expect it to. Customer requirements change. Competitors respond to our initiatives with unanticipated changes in price, products, and incentives. New opportunities and new markets for products appear out of nowhere. Thus, the fledgling company that sticks stubbornly to its initial strategy will find itself in trouble. "Smart entrepreneurs," says Kuemmerle, "recognize that a new venture gains credibility more by simply surviving than by doggedly following its original strategy. They are quick to recognize when they have to change course, and they seldom hesitate to do so."[3]

Know How to Close a Deal

Successful entrepreneurs, says Kuemmerle, understand how to seal a deal. "However tough the market or small the transaction, they know exactly what they must give up—and what they can get away with—while finalizing deals under pressure."[4]

Compared with established corporate managers, the entrepreneur deal maker must be comfortable with risk and must not be intimidated by a shortage of information. Unlike their corporate counterparts, entrepreneurs are much more likely to find themselves in situations in which making a sale, landing a contract, or reaching agreement with a lender means the difference between survival and bankruptcy. They are so close to the edge of failure that every deal has major consequences. Whereas the corporate manager will say, "I'd like more information before I make a decision or make a deal," the entrepreneur must make the best of uncertainty and press forward. Standing still and waiting for more information is less often an option.

Give some thought to where you stand in terms of these entrepreneurial characteristics. Are you comfortable stretching the rules? Are you willing to go up against powerful competitors if necessary? Are you prepared to start small and see how the game plays out before going full speed ahead? If your initial plan runs into a brick wall, are you sufficiently flexible and humble to say, "This isn't working; I need to try something else"? Are you the kind of person who recognizes what must be done—and then does it? If you answered yes to these questions, it's likely that you're entrepreneurial material. If you answered no to more than one, consider how that response could hold you back.

Other Valuable Traits

Kuemmerle's list of personal qualities should be included in every self-diagnosis. But there are others to consider. Entrepreneurs should bring other qualities to the venture:

• Negotiating skills

• Technical skills

• The ability to sell their vision to others, including employees and capital providers

• The ability to motivate employees and delegate work to them

• A knack for turning plans into action—that is, the ability to execute

• A passion for what they are doing

Of those, the last may be the most important, because passion can sustain a person through the long hours and inevitable disappointments that are part of every start-up venture. As Sam Walton used to tell people, "I think I overcame every single one of my personal shortcomings by the sheer passion I brought to my work. I don't know if you're born with this kind of passion, or if you can learn it. But I do know you need it. If you love your work, you'll be out there every day trying to do it the best you possibly can, and pretty soon everybody around will catch the passion from you—like a fever."

SOURCE: Wal-Mart Web site, <www.walmartstores.com/Home Page/About Wal-Mart/The Wal-Mart Culture/Sam's Rules For Building A Business> (accessed 23 March 2004).

Background

Entrepreneurship runs in families to a surprising degree. Children of business owners are more likely than others to start or purchase their own enterprises. Similarly, anecdotal data indicates that children of business-owning parents are more likely than others to enroll in the entrepreneurship courses offered by undergraduate and M.B.A. programs.

This should not be surprising. The challenges, the joys, the difficult choices, and the rewards of business ownership are frequent topics of discussion around the dinner tables of business-owning families. The children learn the "what" and "how" of enterprise ownership from these discussions and from many weekends and summers working in the family store or factory. Indeed, Paul Newman, whom most think of simply as an accomplished actor, grew up in a business-owning family and has recounted in interviews the many childhood weekends he spent in his father's store. Those experiences surely had something to do with his founding of Newman's Own, a packaged food products company whose profits are donated to charity.

Jim Koch, founder and chairman of Boston Beer Company, represents the sixth generation of brewing in his family. Similarly, Dan Bricklin came from a family that owned and ran its own business, and that background surely influenced the future course of his life:

> *My father headed up the family printing business, Bricklin Press, which had been founded by his father in the 1930s. Afternoons spent at the printing plant and dinners devoted to the day's business problems prepared me . . . for the trials I would face in my own business ventures. . . . Growing up, I never expected that some big company would eventually take care of me; instead, I was always looking for opportunities to turn some nifty ideas into a business.*[5]

It May Be Right for You

No matter what your background, an entrepreneurial venture may be right for you. Successful enterprise is a combination of personal qualities and quality planning. You don't have to be a genius with a killer idea: Most successful start-ups begin with incremental innovations. You don't have to be totally fearless: Entrepreneurs who prosper have a healthy aversion to risk. Nor is technical business know-how essential: You can learn as you go along or enlist an experienced business person as a co-owner. An individual who has all the right qualities for entrepreneurial work but a poor plan will not succeed. Nor will a person with a great plan but weak motivation and a terror of uncertainty.

What you must have is a solid plan, the ability to execute it, and a high degree of motivation—motivation that makes business success an important personal goal. Do you have these qualities?

Summing Up

- Ideas are an important element of success for entrepreneurs, but they're not as important as personal background, motivation, and attitude.

- Tests have been designed to measure a person's suitability for an entrepreneurial life, but these tests should be used only as a rough gauge.

- One researcher believes that the following traits are essential for entrepreneurial success: comfort in stretching the rules; being prepared to make powerful enemies; having the patience to start small; a willingness to change strategy quickly; and knowing how to close a deal.

- Entrepreneurship runs in families. Children of business owners are more likely than others to start or purchase their own enterprises.

Finding and Evaluating the Opportunity

Is It Real and Large Enough?

Key Topics Covered in This Chapter

- *five characteristics of a genuine business opportunity*

- *where to look for profitable opportunities*

- *the process of opportunity evaluation*

F RED MANAGED THE service department of a large automobile dealer of Japanese cars. With five years on the job as manager and many more as a mechanic, Fred understood the economics of the auto service business, and he saw what might be an opportunity.

"We're selling more and more hybrid engine cars," he told his brother at a family gathering. "The national organization estimates that hybrids will account for thirty to forty percent of our unit sales three years from now. And two other automakers are moving into hybrids. I think that these gasoline-electric hybrids will define the automobile market for the next twenty years or so, until fuel cell technology or some other technology is commercialized."

"How's that going to affect your service department?" the brother asked.

"Quite a bit," Fred responded. "We've already brought in new diagnostic machines and trained people on hybrid electronic systems and power trains—which are substantially different than those of traditional cars. And we'll be very busy in the years ahead, since we'll get *all* the repair and maintenance business on these cars for the foreseeable future, even after warranties have expired. Traditional mechanics don't know how to work on hybrids, and many will never learn."

Later that day, Fred reflected on this conversation. "There may be an opportunity here," he told himself. After new hybrid vehicle warranties expired, he reasoned, owners would have no options for repair and maintenance except high-priced dealer service departments like his. Neighborhood mechanics wouldn't be equipped or trained to deal with these cars for many years. Many owners would welcome a lower-priced alternative—one that specialized in the repair and maintenance of hybrid engine vehicles.

With his experience and knowledge of service department costs to guide him, Fred began to measure the breadth of his newfound business opportunity. He had industry estimates of hybrid vehicle sales; he knew which diagnostic and other equipment was needed—and what it cost; and he was intimately familiar with the cost of running a fully staffed service facility. He began putting these numbers together, and his optimism grew as he did so. Before long, Fred was envisioning a high-quality service center called The Hybrid Auto Care Center. And if that proved successful, he could foresee a chain of cloned outlets—perhaps a national franchise.

Fred had recognized a business opportunity, the first step in the entrepreneurship process. This chapter will help you explore it.

Characteristics of an Opportunity

Entrepreneurial people are always generating ideas for potential businesses. But how can they sift through these ideas and recognize the few that represent true business opportunities? One way to begin is to define the characteristics of a genuine opportunity.

Jeffry Timmons, a leading expert on entrepreneurship, has described an opportunity as a product or service that

1. creates significant value for customers by solving a significant problem or filling a significant unmet need for which they are willing to pay a premium

2. offers significant profit potential to the entrepreneur and investors—enough to meet their risk/reward expectations

3. represents a good fit with the capabilities of the founder and the management team—that is, something they have the experience and skills to pursue[1]

4. is durable in the sense that the opportunity for profits will persist over a reasonable length of time—that is, is not based on a momentary fad or need that will quickly disappear[2]

We add a fifth characteristic to this commendable list, this one suggested by Alfred E. Osborne Jr., director of UCLA's Price Center for Entrepreneurial Studies:

5. The opportunity is amenable to financing. One would think that a promising commercial idea would always find financial backing, but experience teaches us otherwise.

Now let's examine each segment of this definition in detail.

Creating Value

Customers will pay for a product or service only if they perceive a benefit whose value exceeds its cost. And the greater the perceived value, the more they will pay. CEMEX, a global producer of cement and ready-mixed cement, does not have a unique product or service. Cement is a commodity product. Construction companies can phone almost any cement company and schedule the delivery of ready-mixed cement to their building sites. The only problem is that delivery is often unreliable, or the vendor can promise delivery only within a three-hour window. Unfortunately, that's not good enough for many customers. A delivery that fails to show up or that makes a construction crew of twenty people stand around waiting creates havoc with the schedule and causes labor costs to escalate.

To create value for its customers, CEMEX adopted a concept popularized by pizza shops: twenty-minute delivery guaranteed, or CEMEX would pay the bill. Its ability to execute this concept has allowed the company to grow and prosper. As described by consultants David Bovet and Joseph Martha, "Cemex offers delivery reliability in an industry that is chronically unreliable. It meets its delivery commitments 90 percent of the time versus the 34 percent commonly achieved by its competitors. This super-reliability allows CEMEX to charge a premium in most markets, contributing to operating profit levels 50 percent higher than those of its key competitors."[3] Yes, even something as mundane as cement can create customer value and become the basis of a competitive enterprise,

Significant Profit Potential

To qualify as an opportunity, a business must offer the potential for significant profit. But what is "significant"? Each person will have a different view. The person seeking a lifestyle business will look for something capable of providing a comfortable livelihood—perhaps one that can be passed on to children as they mature. Truly ambitious entrepreneurs and their financial backers will seek much more. For them, significant profit potential is likely to be a business capable of turning a profit within two or three years, $10 million in sales within five years, with a 10–12 percent profit margin, and, if all goes well, 20 percent annual revenue growth over the next five years. Anything with less potential may not interest them.

Risk must play a part in every consideration of profit opportunity because the two tend to go hand in hand. Corporate employees often fret about workplace insecurity: "I could lose my job if the economy doesn't improve." True, people who are not protected by employment contracts run the risk of being fired or furloughed. For the people who start new businesses, however, the risks are much, much higher. If things don't work out, they lose both their employment *and* the personal savings they've invested. Investors are similarly at risk; in the worst case they can lose 100 percent of their invested capital. Given the high risks of entrepreneurship, there should be correspondingly high potential rewards associated with an opportunity.

There is a very real trade-off between risk and return, as shown in figure 2-1. Notice the association between risk and return. Point A in the figure has zero risk and a very low return. Points B, C, and D provide the investor or entrepreneur with rewards commensurate with the risk. Point E—in fact, any point below the diagonal line— is to be avoided because it does not fully reward the investor or entrepreneur for the risks taken. Thus, there's no point in investing in a business that promises no more than a 5 percent return when a person could do almost as well by investing in ten-year U.S. Treasury bonds, which have no default risk.

FIGURE 2-1

The Risk/Return Trade-Off

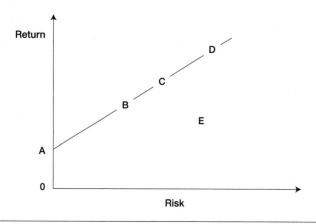

The profit opportunity can be measured by means of a pro forma income statement. (If you are unfamiliar with the income statement or other financial statements used in business, see appendix A.) A pro forma income statement provides a best estimate of future revenues, expenses, and taxes for one or more years. The net result shown on this statement is the anticipated profit, the entrepreneur's measure of opportunity for those years. Because lenders and investors will want to see a set of these statements, let's create a pro forma income statement using The Hybrid Auto Care Center as an example (table 2-1). Here, Fred has forecast results during the first three years of operation.

In Fred's case, the first year of operation shows a net loss of more than $21,000, even though he has earmarked a very small salary for himself. The magnitude of the opportunity grows substantially in succeeding years, however, as the volume of business (i.e., revenues) increases. If volume continues to build in subsequent years, a second facility—if not a regional chain—might be feasible.

Naturally, the opportunity reflected in a pro forma income statement is only as valid as the numbers it contains. A person such as Fred, who conceives of a business that is closely or directly related to his current experience, can usually develop reliable expense num-

TABLE 2-1

The Hybrid Auto Care Center, Pro Forma Income Statement for Years Ending 31 December 2005, 2006, and 2007

	2005	2006	2007
Revenues	$250,000	$450,000	$700,000
Expenses:			
Owner's salary	35,000	50,000	70,000
Employee salaries	70,000	90,000	150,000
Benefits	26,250	35,000	55,000
Workers insurance	7,000	8,000	14,000
Equipment loan 1*	42,000	42,000	42,000
Equipment loan 2**			14,000
Insurance	3,500	3,800	4,000
Shop rent	20,000	20,000	20,000
Utilities	5,500	5,700	6,000
Other	5,000	8,000	15,000
Parts & materials	50,000	90,000	140,000
Advertising	7,000	8,000	9,000
Total expenses	$271,250	$360,500	$539,000
Profits before tax	($21,250)	$89,500	$161,000
Tax	0	26,850	48,300
Profits after tax	($21,250)	$62,650	$112,700

* $300,000 loan@9% 12 years
** $100,000 loan@9% 12 years

bers. Labor and benefits costs, interest expenses, rent costs per square foot, and so forth are within the scope of his experience. Revenue projections are another matter. In the absence of existing customers, revenue figures and revenue growth must be assumed. And therein lies the most dangerous trap for the entrepreneur.

A Good Fit

A *good fit* is a situation in which the entrepreneur and management team have the managerial, financial, and technical capabilities, along

Other Traps for the Intrepid Entrepreneur

An optimistic revenue projection is the most dangerous trap for the prospective business owner, but not the only one. People often underestimate the amount of advertising they must do to show up on customers' radar. Marketing experts warn against single ad strategies. Most people, they say, must see a company's name repeatedly before they will do business with it. Retailer L.L. Bean, for example, figures that it must send six or seven direct mail catalogs before a prospective customer places an order.

Estimating the space and personnel required to operate a business can also be a trap. In manufacturing and retailing, for example, most people will usually look to their assumed level of sales to determine the amount of space and staffing they will require. The link between sales and these other factors may be inaccurate, resulting in the owner's renting too much space and hiring too many people—or the reverse.

with the personal commitment, that are needed to address a business opportunity. Fred, the fictional character in our hybrid car service example, appears to have a good fit with the opportunity he has identified. He already understands the technology and knows how to deal with it. He is also experienced in the management of an auto service business. Like Fred, Young Bill Gates found a good fit when he began his software business at the dawn of the personal computer era. He understood programming, was committed to the emerging computer industry, and had developed a level of management ability and sales sense commensurate with his early-stage business. But not every entrepreneur or manager has a good fit with the opportunity.

Durability

Some opportunities are durable—that is, they are opportunities that business people can exploit over long periods. They are long-lasting and destined to grow over time. The software industry has demonstrated this durability, as has cell phone service. Others are too fleeting to sustain profitability. Do you remember the Pet Rock, the gag-gift phenomenon of the 1970s? For a few months, people all over the United States were buying Pet Rocks for their friends. But that was the end of it. Most opportunities associated with adolescent fads and fashion are equally short-lived. By the time customer requirements are defined and addressed, teenagers have lost interest and moved on to the next new thing.

Teenagers are not the only fickle customers. Consider the U.S. golfing boom of the 1990s. Golf suddenly became very popular with young and middle-aged adults, mostly men. But before you could learn to spell Annika Sorenstam, interest waned. The sport continued to command a sizable spectator audience, but the number of active amateur participants declined every year between 1999 and 2003. Equipment makers and golf course owners around the country felt the pinch, and many went into bankruptcy. Especially hard hit were the municipalities and private clubs that built new or expanded facilities. By the time these links opened for business, the window of commercial opportunity had slammed shut.

Some opportunities lack durability even though demand remains high for a long time. Low barriers to entry create these situations. A visible opportunity with low entry barriers to new competition is a deadly combination. The supply of the product or service can quickly exceed demand, resulting in price reductions and business distress all around.

Financing

By definition, a business opportunity must be amenable to financing. One would think that any promising commercial idea would find financial backing—from the idea generator, friends and family, bankers, and so forth. But experience does not bear this out. Between 2000 and 2004, for example, entrepreneurs in the biotech industry had plenty of ideas for new vaccines and therapies. Several years earlier, these great ideas would have found the financing they needed, but they were starved for financing during the period in question because of a lack of investor confidence.

Before You Leap

When you've identified a business opportunity, size it up in terms of these characteristics.

- Does it create value for its intended customers—enough so that they will pay for it, and hopefully pay a premium price?

- Can you profitably deliver your product or service?

- Is the potential profitability commensurate with the associated business risks?

- Is there a good fit between the opportunity and the capabilities of you and your team?

- Will the window of opportunity stay open long enough for you to exploit it? You must avoid a situation that will evaporate in a short time. You must also avoid situations where competitors can quickly enter the field.

- Is your idea amenable to financing?

Before moving on, ask yourself how well Fred's idea for a hybrid vehicle care center measures up to these definitions of a credible opportunity. Do the same for any opportunities you've been considering.

Where to Look for Opportunities

Opportunities for profitable enterprises are always opening in free-market economies, and alert entrepreneurs are eager to identify them. But where are the best places to look? The answer is to look (1) where things are changing and (2) under the radar of big, powerful companies.

New Knowledge and Technological Change

Enterprise follows in the wake of expanding knowledge and technical change. New knowledge in the field of microbiology, for example, has spawned hundreds of new biotech enterprises and their supplier companies. Technology created in MIT's research labs has produced hundreds of high-tech business start-ups in the Boston area. Meanwhile, in the centuries-old steel industry, Nucor Corporation's success in producing a workable system of continuous casting has led to the rise of new mini-mills.

Regulatory Change

The 1980s deregulation of the U.S. telephone industry—namely, the court-ordered breakup of the AT&T/Bell monopoly—provides a powerful example of how regulatory change creates business opportunities. That set of events created a tidal wave of innovation and new company start-ups, including new long-distance carriers such as Sprint and MCI. Later, dozens of cell phone companies and equipment producers emerged. Similarly, deregulation of the U.S. airline industry produced many regional start-ups, including Southwest Airlines and JetBlue. The same explosion of product and service innovations followed the lifting of government-mandated commission rates in the securities industries of the United States and the United Kingdom.

Social Turmoil and Civic Failure

People want the best for themselves and their children. When the public sector fails in its responsibilities, people often take those responsibilities into their own hands and patronize companies that can help them. Thus, perceptions of rising crime rates and the documented mediocrity of many public school systems have opened a floodgate of opportunities for entrepreneurs—for car alarms, bulletproof vests, home security systems, private schools and child day care, and tutoring systems, to name only a few.

Changing Tastes

Big companies are so invested in their existing products and so consumed with operational details that they are often slow in responding to changing tastes among customers. Their slowness results in unmet needs that entrepreneurs can exploit.

For example, few non-European adults drank wine until the 1960s. But after they developed a taste for it and grew more discerning, opportunities for small, high-quality vintners exploded in the United States, Chile, Australia, and New Zealand. European firms were unable to meet this rising demand. We witness a similar situation today as North Americans and populations in northern Europe are beginning to recognize the nutritional and culinary benefits of olive oil, a staple of the heart-healthy Mediterranean diet. Olive oil consumption in the United States has been racing ahead at roughly a 20 percent annual growth rate as consumers move away from butter, margarine, and other cooking fats. This change is opening opportunities for quality olive oil producers such as Long Meadow Ranch and McAvoy Ranch in northern California, Hacienda La Laguna outside Baeza, Spain, and many other new producers around the globe.

Entrepreneurs can spot such opportunities by watching trendsetters: outstanding chefs, upwardly mobile and highly educated young adults, and cutting-edge health care providers. Their choices and recommendations to others often contain the seeds of broadbased trends.

The Quest for Convenient Solutions

Modern urban life has provided many households with substantial discretionary income but has robbed them of discretionary time. Particularly in Japan and the United States, where vacation days are few and leisure hours are eaten up by commuting and chores, people are receptive to convenient solutions to life's annoyances. They will gladly pay someone for servicing the car, cleaning the house, steam-cleaning the carpets, preparing meals, giving the dog a midday walk, providing after-school child care, painting and decorating, and on and on. Up until the early twentieth century, middle-class U.S. families employed live-in servants—usually immigrant girls—to handle these many chores. Today they outsource those tasks to entrepreneurial caterers, pet and lawn care companies, grocery delivery services (e.g., Peapod), house cleaning specialists, and so forth. How many of these enterprises do you patronize today? Can you think of convenient solutions that you could provide to households like yours?

Under the Radar

Another place to look for promising opportunities is under the radar of big companies. Consider the plight of one enterprising corporate middle manager. She has just discovered an opportunity for a new line of business, which she has taken to her boss, the vice president of product development for Gigantic Electronics Corporation. The first words out of his mouth are straightforward: "What's the revenue potential of this business five years from now?"

"I'm estimating eight million to ten million dollars by the end of year five," she says.

"That's chump change to us," he laughs. "Talk to me again when you have something with a revenue potential of a hundred million or more. Anything less is too small for us."

The VP isn't necessarily being arrogant or short-sighted; huge corporations are handicapped in dealing with what are, to them, small business opportunities. Their human and physical assets are configured to address large markets. Thus, many worthy projects are rejected. These discarded opportunities, however, may be gold mines for small, entrepreneurial businesses. In fact, many managers and engineers leave their companies to exploit projects that their employers have rejected as too small.

Ironically, the big, inflexible corporations that will not pursue small, entrepreneurial ventures often end up writing huge checks to acquire these same ventures after they are successful and have grown substantially. The case of Snapple is instructive. Snapple was an entrepreneurial firm that developed a very successful ice-tea and fruit-drink business. And it was growing fast. Between 1991 and 1994, its revenues skyrocketed from $95 million to $516 million. Instead of starting its own ice-tea and fruit-drink enterprise, U.S. food giant Quaker, a unit of PepsiCo, acquired Snapple in 1994 for $1.7 billion.

Avoid This Mistake

Many people confuse their personal interests with real business opportunities. For example, Sheila loves to ski in the winter and bicycle during the rest of the year. She has a passion for these activities and substantial expertise in selecting, using, and repairing the equipment. She is also unhappy with her job as a securities analyst. So Sheila is thinking about opening a ski/bicycle shop in a small town in Vermont, near her favorite ski area. "If this works out," she tells herself, "I might be able to expand to other ski areas in New England."

Sheila's passion for skiing and biking is a big plus. Passion and commitment make it possible for business owners to put in the long days that success requires. But is there a significant unmet demand for her goods and services? Does this business have real profit potential? Does she have the experience or know-how to successfully manage a retail store? These are fundamental questions that many would-be entrepreneurs fail to ask—or answer—before leaping in. Thus, we see people opening bookstores because they like being around books and the people who read them. Other people open pet stores because they love animals.

A passion for a product or service is wonderful, but it's no substitute for a sound business opportunity.

From Identification to Evaluation

Identifying an opportunity is only the first step in the entrepreneurial process. The next is evaluation, whose purpose is to reveal the scope and details of the perceived opportunity. To be systematic in your evaluation, follow these steps:

1. Begin with a thorough examination of the market for the business's product or service.

2. Assess the current and anticipated level of competition and define the strategy that would give you an edge.

3. Look at the economics of the opportunity.

4. Consider the financial and human resources required for success.

The Market

Many entrepreneurs are so excited about what their new gizmo or service can do that they forget to assess its value to customers. But in the end, the business can succeed only if enough people recognize that value and are willing to pay for it. Thus, the entrepreneur should begin by asking customer and market questions, such as the following. Try to answer each of these questions about an opportunity you've identified.

- How will it benefit customers? *tool for entertainment.*

- How many people stand to benefit? In other words, what is the size of the market? *(4M) age= 18+* *4M x 602= population size of mkt.*

- Is the market stable or growing? If it's growing, at what annual rate? *growing. annual rate=?*

- What percentage of the total market could the product (service) reasonably hope to capture over the next few years?

- Is another product or service from competitors available to fill part of this demand? *yes. - Yelp* *- Yahoo tour.* *- Daily Bulletin* *(e.(A Group Newsppers.*

- Are potential customers aware of their need for this product (or service), or is the need latent—that is, an undiscovered need? *- undiscovered need.*

- Who exactly are the potential customers? Can you name them? Can you describe them? If you cannot, perhaps your business opportunity is strictly theoretical. *-families -college students -moms -commuters* *- young -teens -Nadas 18+ -(peau 18+* *- usiter.*

- How can you reach the potential customers and make a transaction—directly, through distributors, or through retail stores?

- What is the utility of the product (or service) relative to substitutes? For example, a cell phone provides telephone service when customers are moving from place to place. But users of landline phones don't need a second line to handle DSL service.

all in the mission statement *^yellow pgs=sub* *-info is organized in a way that is easy to get to.*

Hopefully, you were able to answer each of the previous questions without too much head-scratching. If you cannot, it's time to start digging for the answers.

Let's consider how our hypothetical new venture, Fred's Hybrid AutoCare Center, might fare in this type of assessment. Table 2-2 shows how Fred might have sized up his opportunity.

The Competitive Situation

Now try to answer the next set of questions. These address the competitive situation. If you're entering an existing market, you'll be up

TABLE 2-2

Market Evaluation for The Hybrid Auto Care Center

Customer benefit	• Lower price than equivalent service at the dealer • Greater expertise. We service only hybrid-powered vehicles and have all the right equipment.
Market size	• Currently (2004) 220,000 vehicles on the road—Toyotas and Hondas. Ford planning to enter the market beginning 2005; GM and DaimlerChrysler to follow in 2006–2007. Industry estimates point to 1.7 million on the road by 2007, and 2.6 million by 2010.
Market growth rate	• As of 2004, calculated at 23 percent compound annual rate.
Market share	• Share of service business within a 20-mile radius estimated at 18 percent during the first five years.
Competitors	• Main competition would be dealers, who would get most of the business during warranty periods. • Other new hybrid specialty shops likely to open to service the rising demand. • Few neighborhood garages would have the training or equipment to provide service.
Customer awareness of need	• Will become obvious as warranty periods expire and the high cost of dealer service becomes clear.
Customers	• All owners of hybrid-powered vehicles of all makes and models.
Reaching customers	• Advertising to list of hybrid owners in the service area • Free informational owner clinics ("Understanding Your Hybrid Vehicle")
Product utility	• Cost and quality

against competitors. Some may be entrenched and capable. If your market is new and attractive, you can be sure that it will attract other profit-seekers—like you.

- How are customers currently satisfying the need you've identified (e.g., with a landline phone instead of a cell phone)?

- What are the strengths and weakness of the main competitors (e.g., high quality, poor customer service, high price)? *look e lAdoc*

- How would a smart competitor respond to your entering the *-reduce price -expand thier* market (e.g., by reducing price, making product improvements)? *listings. -sabotage*

- Are the barriers to market entry high or low? Low barriers *low.* usually mean that competitors will continue to enter the market until returns are driven to a low level. If entry barriers are high, how will you surmount them?

- Have current competitors shown themselves to be agile and responsive to customer needs and technical change? *Daily Brillehps =yes. Recent site update (2008)*

- What is the single *worst* thing that a competitor could do to your business prospects (e.g., drop the price 20 percent)? When you've answered this question, think about how that worst *apples ut afront* thing would affect your prospects for success and how you would respond. What strategy on pricing, positioning, service, *going mobile lwel app* distribution, or product features would give you a sustainable *for itnes/ iuscle/PDA/ smartphons.* competitive advantage?

You should thoroughly examine and satisfactorily answer each of these questions with documentation. If you will be seeking outside capital, those documented answers are essential.

Underlying Economics

Every business rests on an economic structure, and that structure influences its ability to compete and succeed. Some businesses—such as supermarkets—have a very low *profit margin* on sales, but the successful ones have very large sales volumes. (Expressed as a percentage, profit margin is profit divided by sales revenue.) On the other

profit margin = profit ÷ revenue
rev

end of the spectrum, we have, for example, custom furniture makers who don't sell many items but generally make a large profit on each sale. What is the profit structure of your business opportunity?

Think too about the cost structure of the proposed business. Some businesses operate with high fixed costs and low variable costs. *Fixed costs* are costs that stay about the same no matter how many goods or services are produced. For example, an automobile engine plant has high fixed costs—for debt payments, insurance, specialized equipment, and salaried supervisors. These costs remain roughly the same whether the plant produces one hundred engines per year or ten thousand. *Variable costs*, in contrast, are those that rise or fall with the level of output. These include the cost of materials, energy, and, in many cases, labor. It is important to understand these costs because (1) they will help you understand the basis of profitability, and (2) if you know the revenues you'll receive from each unit sale, you will be able to determine the *breakeven point* of your operations—that is, the number of units you'll have to sell before you earn a profit. (See Appendix B for an explanation of the breakeven point and information on how to calculate it.)

Enterprises with high fixed costs and low variable costs (e.g., high-volume manufacturers) generally have high breakeven points but enjoy high profitability on sales after they get past that point. Those with low fixed costs and high variable costs (e.g., a technical service firm) have low breakeven points but relatively low profitability on sales thereafter.

Understanding the economics of a business opportunity is critically important. The next set of questions will help you think through and evaluate the economics of your opportunity. Try to provide a complete answer to each.

- Will the business be a price setter or a price taker? What are the constraints on pricing what the business sells? *[PIS stardt — impressions]*

- What is the supply/demand situation relative to your product or service? *no immediate demand.*

- Is demand elastic or inelastic—that is, would a price increase by you dramatically reduce buyer demand (elastic), or would demand be only slightly affected (inelastic) in the short run?
  reduce buyer demand if imps went down

The Bottom Line

After you've identified an opportunity and evaluated it in terms of the market, competition, and economic value, ask yourself these two questions:

1. Is it still attractive in terms of the risk/return relationship described in figure 2-1?

2. Is it more or less attractive than other opportunities available to you?

Don't overlook these questions. Always consider the attractiveness of an opportunity relative to others you could pursue—including doing nothing. Remember that leaving your capital in a money-market fund earning an anemic 2 percent interest is an alternative, and one that you can follow until an opportunity with all the right characteristics appears on your radar.

What are the variable costs = resources/labor (marketing)

- What substitutes do prospective customers have for your product or service? *competitors.*

- Will the business be dominated by fixed or variable costs?

- To what extent can suppliers and employees enforce cost increases on the proposed business? *—continuing to uphold the brand and integrity of the site*

Summing Up

- A business opportunity is one that (1) creates significant value for customers, (2) offers significant risk-adjusted profit potential, (3) has a good fit with the capabilities of the management team, (4) is potentially profitable over a reasonable time span, and (5) is amenable to financing.

- To uncover entrepreneurial opportunities, look in areas of (1) new knowledge and technological change, (2) changing regulation, (3) social turmoil and civic failure, and (4) chang-ing tastes. Also seek out opportunities for convenient solutions to people's problems.

- Large companies often reject profitable opportunities because they are "too small." They can be exploited by the enterprising small business.

- Promising opportunities must be systematically evaluated through a process that considers the market, the current and anticipated level of competition, the underlying economics, and the resources required for success.

3

Organizing the Enterprise

Which Form Is Best for You?

Key Topics Covered in This Chapter

- *the various legal forms of organization available to U.S. businesses*

- *the advantages and disadvantages of each form*

- *determining which form is best for your business*

ONE KEY ISSUE that every entrepreneur must address at the onset of a new venture is the legal form the enterprise will adopt. Should it be a sole proprietorship, a partnership, a corporation, a limited liability company?

This decision is driven chiefly by the objectives of the entrepreneur and the firm's investors. But taxation and legal liabilities also play a part. The choice is made difficult by the trade-offs built into the law. To get the most favorable tax treatment, a business must often give up some protection from liability, some flexibility, or both. This chapter provides a brief overview of the choices available to the new enterprise and summarizes the advantages and disadvantages of each.

Sole Proprietorship

The *sole proprietorship* is the oldest, simplest, and most common form of business entity. It is a business owned by a single individual. For tax and legal liability purposes, the owner and the business are one and the same. The proprietorship is not taxed as a separate entity. Instead, the owner reports all income and deductible expenses for the business on Schedule C of the personal income tax return. Note that the earnings of the business are taxed at the individual level, whether or not they are actually distributed in cash. There is no vehicle for sheltering income.

A Note About Legalities

The information given in this chapter is based on U.S. law but should not be considered as legal advice. Always consult with an attorney on these matters. Readers located outside the United States should consult their own legal and tax sources.

For liability purposes, the individual and the business are also one and the same. Thus, legal claimants can pursue the personal property of the proprietor and not simply the assets used in the business.

Advantages of a Sole Proprietorship

Perhaps the greatest advantage of this form of business is its simplicity and low cost. You are not required to file with the government, although some businesses, such as restaurants and child day care centers, must be licensed by local health or regulatory authorities. Nor is any legal charter required. The owner can simply begin doing business.

The sole proprietorship form of business has other advantages:

- The owner or proprietor is in complete control of business decisions.

- The income generated through operations can be directed into the proprietor's pocket or reinvested as he or she sees fit.

- Profits flow directly to the proprietor's personal tax return; they are not subject to a second level of taxation. In other words, profits from the business will not be taxed at the business level.

- The business can be dissolved as easily and informally as it was begun.

These advantages account for the widespread adoption of the sole proprietorship in the United States. Any person who wants to set up shop and begin dealing with customers can get right to it, in most cases without the intervention of government bureaucrats or lawyers.

Disadvantages of the Sole Proprietorship

This legal form of organization, however, has disadvantages:

- The amount of capital available to the business is limited to the owner's personal funds and whatever funds can be borrowed. This disadvantage limits the potential size of the business, no matter how attractive or popular its product or service.

- Sole proprietors have unlimited liability for all debts and legal judgments incurred in the course of business. Thus, a product liability lawsuit by a customer will not be made against the business but rather against the owner.

- The business may not be able to attract high-caliber employees whose goals include a share of business ownership. Sharing the benefits of ownership, other than simple profit-sharing, would require a change in the legal form of the business.

- Some employee benefits, such as owner's life, disability, and medical insurance premiums, may not be deductible—or may be only partially deductible—from taxable income.

- The entity has a limited life; it exists only as long as the owner is alive. Upon the owner's death, the assets of the business go to his or her estate.

- As you will see later in this book, venture capitalists and other outside investors of equity capital will not participate in a sole proprietorship business.

Partnership

A *partnership* is a business entity having two or more owners. In the United States a partnership is treated as a proprietorship for tax and liability purposes. Earnings are distributed according to the partner-

Tips for Starting a Sole Proprietor Business

You can start a sole proprietorship by simply going to it: by offering your services as a consultant, buying and reselling merchandise, writing a subscription newsletter, and so forth. It's simple. Here are some useful tips:

- Keep your household and business finances separate. You can do that by setting up a separate bank account for your business; run all the business's checks and receipts through that account.

- Use Quicken or a computer spreadsheet to keep track of the many business expenses you'll encounter during the tax year. If you track them under the same categories used in the business expenses section of IRS form Schedule C, it will be simple to itemize these expenses and deduct them from taxable income. And save every receipt!

- If you run the business under a name other than your own— e.g., Surfside Management Consulting—you may need to file a "fictitious name" or "doing business as" certificate in the city where the business is domiciled. And make sure that the name is not already taken by another business.

- Most U.S. states prohibit the use of the words *Corporation, Corp., Incorporated, Inc.*—and even *Company* and *Co.*—after the business's name if it is not incorporated.

ship agreement and are treated as personal income for tax purposes. Thus, like the sole proprietorship, the partnership is simply a conduit for directing income to its partners, as in this example:

Bill and Bob formed a partnership and started a restaurant called The Billy-Bob Café. By agreement, they split the profits of the business equally, the total of which amounted to $140,000 last year. Bill, who had no other source of earnings last year, reported $70,000 in income on his personal tax return. Bob, who earned another $20,000 from a *part-time job, had to report $90,000 on his personal income tax return ($70,000 in partnership income plus $20,000 from his other job).*

Partnerships have a unique liability situation. Each partner is jointly and severally liable. Thus, a damaged party can pursue a single partner or any number of partners—and that claim may or may not be proportional to the invested capital of the partners or the distribution of earnings. This means that if Bill did something to damage a customer, that customer could sue both Bill *and* Bob even though Bob played no part in the problem.

Organizing a partnership is not as effortless as with a sole proprietorship. The partners must determine, and should set down in writing, their agreement on a number of issues:

- The amount and nature of their respective capital contributions (e.g., one partner might contribute cash, another a patent, and a third property and cash)

- How the business's profits and losses will be allocated

- Salaries and draws against profits

- Management responsibilities

- The consequences of withdrawal, retirement, disability, or the death of a partner

- The means of dissolution and liquidation of the partnership

Advantages of a Partnership

Partnerships have many of the same advantages of the sole proprietorship, along with others:

- Except for the time and the legal cost of crafting a partnership agreement, it is easy to establish.

- Because there is more than one owner, the entity has more than one pool of capital to tap in financing the business and its operations.

- Profits from the business flow directly to the partners' personal tax returns; they are not subject to a second level of taxation.

- The entity can draw on the judgment and management of more than one person. In the best cases, the partners will have complementary skills.

Disadvantages of a Partnership

As mentioned earlier, partners are jointly and severally liable for the actions of the other partners. Thus, one partner can put other partners at risk without their knowledge or consent. Other disadvantages include the following:

- Profits must be shared among the partners.

- With two or more partners being privy to decisions, decision making may be slower and more difficult than in a sole proprietorship. Disputes can tie the partnership in knots.

- As with a sole proprietorship, the cost of some employee benefits may not be deductible from income taxation.

- Depending on the partnership agreement, the partnership may have a limited life. Unless otherwise specified, it will end upon the withdrawal or death of any partner.

The Limited Partnership

The type of partnership entity described thus far is legally referred to as a general partnership. It is what we normally think of when describing a partnership. There is another partnership form, however, that you should understand: the *limited partnership*. This is a hybrid form of organization having both limited and general partners. The general partner (there may be more than one) assumes management responsibility and unlimited liability for the business and must have at least a 1 percent interest in profits and losses. The limited partner (or partners) has no voice in management and is legally liable only for the amount of his or her capital contribution plus any other debt obligations specifically accepted.

The usual motive behind a limited partnership is to bring together individuals who have technical or management expertise (the general partners) and well-heeled investors who know little about the business—or who lack the time to participate—but who wish to participate in an opportunity for financial gain.

Note that in a limited partnership, profits and losses can be allocated differently among the partners. That is, even if profits are allocated 20 percent to the general partner and 80 percent to the limited partners, the limited partners may get 99 percent of the losses. (Well-heeled limited partners often favor this arrangement when they can use the partnership's losses to offset taxable earnings from other sources.) Losses, however, are deductible only up to the amount of capital at risk. The distribution of profit is subject to all sorts of creative structuring, such as those observed in certain venture capital and real estate partnerships. In some of those arrangements, the limited partners get 99 percent of the profits until they have gotten back an amount equal to their entire capital contributions, at which point the general partner begins to receive 30 percent and the limited partners' share drops to 70 percent.

C Corporations

The *C corporation* is synonymous with the common notion of a corporation. When a business incorporates, it becomes a C corporation unless it makes a special election to become an S corporation, which is described later in this chapter. C corporations in the United States are vastly outnumbered by sole proprietorships, and yet they account for almost 90 percent of all U.S. sales. This is because the vast majority of the nation's major companies are corporations.

In the United States, a corporation is an entity chartered by the state and treated as a person under the law. This means that it can sue and be sued; it can be fined and taxed by the state; and it can enter into contracts. The C corporation can have an infinite number of owners. Ownership is evidenced by shares of company stock. The entity is managed on behalf of shareholders—at least indirectly—by a board of directors.

The corporate form is appealing to entrepreneurs for several reasons. First, in contrast to the sole proprietorship, the C corporation's owners are personally protected from liability. To appreciate this protection, consider the case of the massive oil spill of the oil tanker *Exxon Valdez* in 1989. Even if the damages against Exxon had exceeded the company's net worth, the courts could not have pursued the company's individual shareholders for further damages. An individual owner's liability is limited to the extent of his or her investment in the firm. This corporate shell, or veil, can be pierced only in the event of fraud.

Another appealing feature is the corporation's ability to raise capital. Unlike the sole proprietorship and partnership, which must rely on a single owner or small number of partners for equity capital, a corporation has the potential to tap the capital of a vast number of investors: individuals as well as institutions, such as pension funds and mutual funds. Equity (or ownership) capital is contributed by shareholders when they purchase stock issued directly from the company. In return they receive a fractional ownership share in the assets and future fortunes of the company. A successful and growing company can often raise capital through successive public offerings of its stock. The corporation can also borrow money.

Advantages of the C Corporation

The advantages of the C corporation, then, can be summarized as follows:

- Shareholders have limited liability for the corporation's debts and judgments against it. Officers, however, can be held personally liable for their actions, such as the failure to withhold and pay corporate taxes.

- Corporations can raise funds through the sale of stock.

- Corporations can deduct the cost of certain benefits they provide to officers and employees.

- Theoretically, a corporation has an unlimited life span.

- Because a corporation can compensate employees with company shares, it is in a better position than proprietorships and partnerships to attract and retain talent.

- Ownership shares are transferable. Shareholders can sell some or all of their interests in the company (assuming that there's a market for them). They can also give their shares to family members or charities.

Disadvantages of the C Corporation

As if to remind us that we cannot have our cake and eat it, the C corporation has several clear disadvantages. Perhaps the greatest is the problem of double taxation. The C corporation is taxed on its earnings (profits). Whatever is left over after taxes can be distributed to shareholders in the form of dividends or can be retained in the business to finance operations or growth. But consider what happens to after-tax dividends that are distributed to shareholders. These dividends must be reported by shareholders as taxable dividend income. Thus, earnings are taxed twice: once at the corporate level and again at the shareholder level.

(Note: Dividend income is taxed in the United States at a lower rate than in the past. Beginning in 2003, qualified dividends are subject to the same 5 percent or 15 percent maximum tax rate that applies to net capital gain. Before 2003, all dividends were taxed at the higher tax rates that applied to ordinary income.)

To understand this double-taxation problem, consider this example:

Amalgamated Hat Rack earned $647,500 before taxes and paid a little more than 46 percent of this ($300,000) in state and federal corporate income taxes, leaving it with $347,500 in after-tax profit. If the company paid $10,000 of that in the form of a dividend to Angus McDuff, its founder and CEO, McDuff would be required to add that amount to his personal taxable income, which might be taxed by both the state and *the federal government. Thus, the same income is taxed twice. (Note: There is a minor exception to this double-taxation issue in the case of corporations that receive dividend income from other corporations.)*

Other disadvantages include the following:

- The process of incorporation is often costly. The corporation must create a set of rules for governing the entity, including stockholder meetings, board of directors meetings, the election of officers, and so forth.

- Corporations are monitored by federal, state, and some local agencies. Public corporations must publish their results quarterly.

For the entrepreneur, adoption of the corporate form is a way to "liquefy" his or her personal equity in the company; paper wealth can be turned into real money. And it is a great way to raise the capital needed for growth. But every share sold dilutes the entrepreneur's ownership and personal control.

S Corporations

The *S corporation* is another creature of U.S. tax law. It is a closely held corporation whose tax status is the same as the partnership's, but its participants enjoy the liability protections granted to corporate shareholders. In other words, it is a conduit for passing profits and losses directly to the personal income tax returns of its shareholders, whose legal liabilities are limited to the amount of their capital contributions.

In exchange for these favorable treatments, the law places a number of restrictions on the types of corporations that can elect S status. To qualify for S corporation status, an organization must meet the following requirements:

- Have only one class of stock, although differences in voting rights are allowed

- Be a domestic corporation, owned wholly by U.S. citizens, and derive no more than 80 percent of its revenues from non–U.S. sources

- Have thirty-five or fewer stockholders (husbands and wives count as one stockholder)

- Derive no more than 25 percent of revenues from passive sources, such as interest, dividends, rents, and royalties

- Have only individuals, estates, and certain trusts as shareholders (i.e., no corporations or partnerships)

The last provision excludes venture capitalists as potential shareholders because most venture-capitalist firms are partnerships.

The Limited Liability Company

The limited-liability company (LLC) is a relatively new type of entity designed to afford the same benefits as does the S corporation. The LLC is similar to an S corporation in that it enjoys the tax advantages of a partnership and the liability protections of a corporation. Although state laws differ somewhat, an LLC is like an S corporation but with none of the restrictions on the number or type of participants. Owners are neither proprietors, partners, nor shareholders; instead, they are "members."

The LLC is similar to a partnership in that the LLC's operating agreement (the equivalent of a partnership agreement) may distribute profits and losses in a variety of ways, not necessarily in proportion to capital contributions. Law firms are often organized as LLCs.

Aside from its taxation and limited liabilities protections, the LLC is simple to operate; like a sole proprietorship, for example, there is no statutory requirement to keep minutes, hold meetings, or make resolutions—requirements that often trip up corporation owners.

Which Form Makes Sense for You?

As you have no doubt gathered, tax implications are an important factor in the choice of a business entity. Indeed, the incentives of the U.S. tax code give rise to certain tactics that can be risky. For example, the aforementioned double taxation of a corporation's distributed earnings provides an incentive for owner-employees to pay all profits to themselves as compensation. Unlike dividends, compensation is deductible as an expense to the corporation and thus is not taxed twice. However, the Internal Revenue Service (IRS) has certain rules on what is considered reasonable compensation; these rules are designed to discourage just such behavior.

Note too that the tax on individuals in so-called flow-through entities such as partnerships and LLCs is on the income *earned* and not on the actual cash distributed. The income of the partnership is taxed at the personal level of the partners, whether or not any cash is actually distributed. Thus, earnings retained in the business to finance growth or to create a monetary nest egg are taxed even though they are not distributed to the owners.

If the venture is projected to create large losses in the early years, then there may be some benefit to passing those losses through to investors, assuming that the investors are in a position to use them to offset other income and thus reduce their taxes. This situation would favor the partnership or LLC. Similarly, if the business intends to generate substantial cash flow and return it to investors as the primary means of creating value for investors, then a partnership or LLC is still attractive. If, however, the business will require cash investment over the long term and if value is intended to be harvested through a sale or public offering, then a C corporation is the most attractive option.

Of course, a business may move through many forms in its lifetime. A sole proprietorship may become a partnership and finally a C corporation. A limited partnership may become an LLC and then a C corporation. Each transition, however, requires considerable legal work and imposes an administrative burden on the management and owners of the firm. The advantages of the right form of organization at each stage certainly may warrant these burdens. On the other hand, high-potential ventures on the fast track should avoid losing time and focus by jumping through these hoops. For them, the corporate form is almost always best. As corporations, they can use stock and options to lure an experienced management team and to conserve cash. They can even use stock in lieu of all-cash arrangements in paying for consulting services. Also, venture capitalists (VCs) may not take them seriously if they are not incorporated, because VCs will want a block of ownership.

Consequently, if you are an entrepreneur, consider the likely evolution of your business before selecting a particular form of organization, and consult with a qualified tax attorney or accountant before making this important choice.

Summing Up

Table 3-1 summarizes this chapter by outlining the types of businesses discussed here.

TABLE 3-1

Forms of Business

Form of Business	Key Benefits	Key Disadvantages
Sole proprietorship	• Simple to organize and operate • One level of taxation	• Full liability of the owner • Cannot raise outside equity capital, thus limiting potential size of the business
Partnership	• Can bring in additional talent and personal capital • One level of taxation	• Full liability of partners • Capital limited to the pockets of the partners and their ability to borrow • Unless addressed through the partnership agreement, dissolves with the death or withdrawal of any partner
C corporation	• Theoretically capable of attracting equity capital through share ownership • Preferred form of venture capitalists • Able to deduct many benefit payments to employees • Shareholders enjoy limited liability	• Complex to set up and operate • Income subject to double taxation
S corporation	• Like a proprietorship and partnership, subject to only one level of taxation • Shareholders enjoy limited liability	• Complex to set up and operate • Limited in the number of shareholders • Venture capitalists cannot be shareholders
Limited partnership	• Limited liability • One level of taxation	• Complex to set up
Limited liability company	• Simpler to set up and operate than a corporation • Limited liability for members • One level of taxation • Infinite number of possible members	• Cannot attract outside equity capital

Building a Business Model and Strategy

How They Work Together

Key Topics Covered in This Chapter

- *how the business model explains the way key components of the enterprise work together to make money*

- *examples of two powerful business models*

- *how strategy can confer competitive advantage*

- *a five-step process for formulating strategy and aligning activities with it*

- *why strategic thinking must be ongoing*

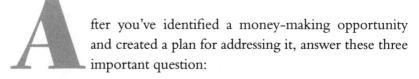

fter you've identified a money-making opportunity and created a plan for addressing it, answer these three important question:

1. How will our new business create value for customers?

2. How will it make a profit for us and our investors?

3. How will the business differentiate itself from competitors?

An entrepreneur should be able to provide concise answers to anyone who asks these questions. If you don't yet have the answers for your business, this chapter's primer on business models and strategy will help you.

Business executives, consultants, and the business media use the terms *business model* and *strategy* casually and generally without rigor. Many, when pressed, cannot define either term. Don't be one of them. As an entrepreneur, you cannot afford fuzzy thinking about these important and very different concepts. As this chapter explains, a business model identifies your customers and describes how your business will profitably address their needs. Strategy, on the other hand, is about differentiating how your business satisfies customers. Both are required for success.

Your Business Model

The term *business model* first came into popular use in the late 1980s, after many people had gained experience with personal computers and spreadsheet software. Thanks to these digital innovations, entrepreneurs and analysts found that they could easily "model" the costs and revenues associated with any proposed business. After the model was set up, it took only a few keystrokes to observe the impact of individual changes—for example, in unit price, profit margin, and supplier costs—on the bottom line. Pro forma financial statements were the primary documents of business modeling. By the time dot-com fever had become rampant, the term *business model* had become a popular buzzword. Still, most people were unable to articulate exactly what it meant.

In the most basic sense, a business model describes how an enterprise proposes to make money. Two Harvard Business School professors—Richard Hamermesh and Paul Marshall—have gone beyond this basic definition. They have defined *business model* as "a summation of the core business decisions and trade-offs employed by a company to earn a profit." The decisions and trade-offs they refer to fall into four groups: *BIZ MODEL TRADE OFFS*

- **Revenue sources.** This money comes from sales, service fees, advertising, and so forth.

- **Cost drivers.** Examples are labor, goods purchased for resale, and energy.

- **Investment size.** Every business needs a measurable level of investment to get off the ground and, in the case of working capital, to keep it operating.

- **Critical success factors.** Depending on the business, a success factor might be the ability to roll out new products on a sustained basis, success in reaching some critical mass of business within a certain time, and so on.[1]

How would you describe your company or business concept in terms of these model elements? Have you nailed down your revenue sources and the factors that will drive costs for your business? Do you know which costs will be fixed and which will vary with sales volume? Have you calculated the capital you'll need to launch and operate the business? What factors are essential for success? Try to answer each of these questions unambiguously, and do so before you approach any investors.

Management consultant Joan Magretta has provided a useful introduction to business models in "Why Business Models Matter," a 2002 *Harvard Business Review* article in which she views a business model as some variation of the value chain that supports every business. "Broadly speaking," she writes, "this chain has two parts. Part one includes all the activities associated with making something: designing it, purchasing raw materials, manufacturing, and so on. Part two includes all the activities associated with selling something: finding and reaching customers, transacting a sale, distributing the product or delivering the service."[2]

How would you describe your enterprise in terms of Magretta's definition? Does your model tell a logical, sensible story? If you were to represent your model on a pro forma income statement with reasonable projections of revenues and expenses, would it be profitable?

Some of today's most powerful and profitable companies grew out of business models that were elegant and compelling in their logic and powerful in financial potential. Let's consider two that are probably familiar to you: Dell Computer and eBay. These examples will help you understand the concept of a business model and its importance.

Example: Dell

Michael Dell went into the personal computer business when Apple, IBM, and a handful of other producers were already established in the market. These manufacturers sold through resellers and maintained large inventories to accommodate the variety of PC features that customers had come to expect. Both practices were costly for the manufacturers, which had to give substantial discounts to resellers. At the same time they took heavy losses in finished-goods inventory whenever the blistering pace of new product introductions made those inventories seem old-fashioned. By one estimate, PCs lost 2 percent of their value each day they sat in the finished-goods storeroom!

Dell's business model avoided both of these profit-sapping problems. As everyone now knows, Dell identified his target market (fairly knowledgeable computer users who needed no hand-holding

[handwritten in left margin: Magretta theory]

by store salesclerks) and sold directly to it, skipping middleman costs. At the same time he designed the business to avoid the cost of finished-goods inventory. His solution was simple: Don't have finished-goods inventory. For the most part, Dell built only machines for which the company had orders (and payments!), and it built those machines to order—a major competitive plus. Dell's finished goods were not sitting in warehouses and losing value in anticipation of customer orders; they were in delivery trucks headed toward waiting customers. The business model facilitated this make-to-order arrangement through a fast and flexible supply chain of component makers and just-in-time assemblers.

One of the more remarkable aspects of the Dell business model was its collection of payments in advance of filling customer orders. There was no 30- to 60-day accounts receivable to be financed with working capital. There were no uncollectibles. Instead, the company turned the traditional cash conversion cycle on its head, receiving customer payments immediately and paying its own suppliers after 30 days.

Example: eBay

eBay, the online auction company, grew out of an even simpler model. Like a telephone company, eBay created an infrastructure that allowed people to communicate—for a modest fee—with each other. Its Web-based infrastructure of software, servers, and rules of behavior allows a community of buyers and sellers to meet and conduct transactions for all manner of goods—from Elvis memorabilia to used Porsches. The company takes no part in the transactions, thereby avoiding many of the costs incurred by other businesses. As described by author David Bunnell, eBay "has no responsibility for goods offered at auction, for collecting buyer's payments, or for shipping. Its only responsibilities are to maintain the integrity of the auction process and the information linkages that make it feasible, and to bill and collect the fees it charges sellers."[3]

As a mechanism for generating income, the eBay model is simple. It receives revenues from seller fees. Those revenues are reduced by the cost of building and maintaining the online infrastructure and by the usual marketing, product development, general, and administrative

costs that keep the operation running and that attract buyers and sellers to the site. The net of these revenues and costs is profits for eBay
shareholders.

Aside from its simplicity, the great power of the eBay model is
the fact that a small number of salaried employees and outsource
partners can handle a huge and growing volume of business. Further, a doubling of transaction volume (and revenue) can be accom-
modated with relatively modest investments. Software and servers do

Testing Your Business Model

How well do you understand the business model of your proposed enterprise? Make sure that the model is clear, complete,
and logical before you invest more time and money. In particular, note these tips:

- Be very clear about your revenue sources and the strength of
  customer attraction to your product or service.

- Map out all tasks that must be accomplished in producing value
  for customers—either by you or by an outsource partner.

- Translate your model into numbers by estimating revenue
  figures and associated costs.

After you've done all these things, use your model as a thinking tool. Look for weaknesses. Ask trusted and experienced
friends for assessments of the model's feasibility. Test its component parts. For example, use market research to verify your revenue estimates; determine the interest of your target customers
in your product or service, and find out what they are willing to
pay for it. If the model calls for outsourcing particular activities
in the value chain, confirm that such outsourcing support is
available at a cost you can afford. Think creatively about how
key tasks in the value chain could be done better—by producing higher perceived quality, greater customer convenience,
faster delivery, or lower cost. In some cases, being distinctively
better at only one key task is the ticket to commercial success.

the heavy lifting. This adds power to the eBay business model. Its heavy reliance on fixed costs over variable costs gives the company enormous operating leverage, allowing the larger part of incremental revenue increases to fall to the bottom line.

Strategy

A business model will help you—and anyone you approach for funding—to understand what your business will do and how all its key parts fit together. But a well-conceived and promising business model is only half the equation for success, because it doesn't take into account the market competition. Dealing with competition is the job of strategy. *Strategy*, in fact, is a plan to differentiate the enterprise and give it a competitive advantage. A successful business has both a solid business model and a good strategy.

Bruce Henderson, founder of Boston Consulting Group, once wrote that competitive advantage is found in differences: "The differences between you and your competitors are the basis of your advantage."[4] Henderson believed that no two competitors could coexist if they sought to do business in the same way. They must differentiate themselves to survive. He wrote, "Each must be different enough to have a unique advantage." For example, two men's clothing stores on the same block—one featuring formal attire and the other focusing on leisure wear—can potentially survive and prosper. However, if the same two stores sold the same things under the same terms, one or the other would perish. More likely, the one that differentiated itself through price, product mix, or ambiance would have the greater likelihood of survival. Harvard Business School professor Michael Porter concurs: "Competitive strategy is about being different. It means deliberately choosing a different set of activities to deliver a unique mix of value."[5] Consider these examples:

- Southwest Airlines didn't become the most profitable air carrier in North America by copying its rivals. It differentiated itself with low fares, frequent departures, point-to-point flights, and customer-pleasing service.

- eBay created an entirely new way for people to sell and acquire new and used goods: online auctions. The company's founders aimed to serve the same purpose as classified ads, flea markets, and formal auctions but made it simple, efficient, and wide-ranging.

- Toyota's strategy in developing the hybrid engine Prius passenger car was to create a competitive advantage within an important segment of auto buyers: people who want a vehicle that is either environmentally benign, cheap to operate, or the latest thing in auto engineering. The company also hoped that the learning associated with the Prius would give it leadership in a technology having huge future potential.

Strategies can be based on low-cost leadership, technical differentiation, or focus. They can also be understood in terms of strategic position. Michael Porter has postulated that strategic positions emerge from three, sometimes overlapping, sources:[6]

- **Variety–based positioning.** Here, a company chooses a narrow subset of product or service offerings from within the wider set offered in its industry. It can succeed with this strategy if it delivers faster, better, or at lower cost than competitors. For example, Starbucks offers premium coffee products and places its outlets in locations that are convenient for potential customers. It doesn't serve breakfast or sell sandwiches. Customers can get those products elsewhere. Its focus is on coffee.

- **Need–based positioning.** Companies that follow this approach, according to Porter, aim to serve all or most of the needs of an identifiable set of customers. These customers may be price sensitive, may demand a high level of personal attention and service, or may want products or services that are uniquely tailored (customized) to their needs. For example, USAA is a financial services company that caters exclusively to active-duty and retired military officers and their families. After decades of serving this population, USAA understands its unique banking,

Fred's Business Model

Recall Fred's plan for The Hybrid Auto Care Center described earlier in this book. Fred, the service manager for a dealer selling the new hybrid autos, sees a profitable business in the repair and maintenance of these gasoline-electric vehicles, especially after their manufacturers' warranties expire. His blueprint is essentially the same one used by auto repair facilities everywhere:

1. Generate customers through local advertising and on-premises information mini-seminars for owners of these unique but increasingly popular vehicles.

2. Have the internal capabilities to diagnose and repair damaged and malfunctioning hybrid engine vehicles of all major manufacturers.

3. Establish a replacement parts pipeline with several regional distributors.

4. Establish outsourcing relationships with a top-quality body shop and an auto air conditioning service company so that personnel can concentrate on mechanical problems.

This is Fred's model for making money. His experience with hybrid repair work and with running a dealer's service department have made him an expert in the details of pricing and cost management. By modeling many different types of repairs on a computer spreadsheet and factoring in known costs for labor, parts, equipment loans, rent, and overhead, he is convinced that he can break even with a crew of five employees and eight thousand "service hours" per year (roughly forty weeks per year). Everything over that breakeven point should produce a profit. He has worked these figures out in a pro forma income statement.

insurance, and retirement needs. And it knows how to deal with the fact that military officers are often transferred from post to post around the world and are often assigned to remote locations for extended periods where they are unable to respond to monthly billings.

- **Access-based positioning.** Some strategies can be based on access to customers. A discount merchandise chain, for example, might choose to locate its stores exclusively in low-income neighborhoods. This reduces competition from suburban shopping malls and provides easy access for its target market of low-income shoppers, many of whom do not have automobiles. Cracker Barrel Old Country Store, in contrast, locates its restaurant/gift stores along the U.S. expressway system, where it caters to travelers. Its Web site even includes a "trip planner" that identifies the locations of all Cracker Barrel outlets along any "to-from" driving route.

What is your strategy for gaining competitive advantage? Will it differentiate your company in ways that attract customers from rivals? Will it draw new customers into the market? Will it give you a tangible advantage?

Simply being different, of course, will not keep you in business; something that is different must be perceived as valuable. And customers define value in different ways: lower cost, greater convenience, greater reliability, faster delivery, or more aesthetic appeal. The list of customer-pleasing "values" is extremely long. What value does your strategy aim to provide? Can it deliver?

Steps for Formulating Strategy

Here are six steps you can follow in formulating a strategy. They involve looking outside and inside your organization, thinking about how you will deal with threats and opportunities as they present themselves, building a good fit with strategy-supporting activities, aligning resources with goals, and organizing for execution.

STEP 1: LOOK OUTSIDE TO IDENTIFY THREATS AND OPPORTU-NITIES. At the highest level, strategy is concerned with analyzing the outside environment and determining how the company's financial resources, people, and capacity should be allocated to create an exploitable advantage. There are always threats in the outside environment: new entrants, demographic changes, suppliers who might cut you off, substitute products that your customers could turn to, and macroeconomic trends that may reduce the ability of your customers to pay. The business you have in mind may be threatened by a competitor that can produce the same quality goods at a much lower price—or a much better product at the same price. A strategy must be able to cope with these threats.

The external environment also harbors opportunities: a new-to-the-world technology, an unserved market, and so forth. So ask yourself these questions:

- What is the economic environment in which we must operate? How is it changing?

- What opportunities for profitable action lie before us?

- What are the risks associated with various opportunities and potential courses of action?

STEP 2: LOOK INSIDE AT RESOURCES, CAPABILITIES, AND PRAC-TICES. Resources and internal capabilities can be a constraint on your choice of strategy, especially for a small start-up with few employees and fixed assets. And rightly so. A strategy to exploit an unserved market in the electronics industry, for example, might not be feasible if your firm lacks the necessary financial capital and the human know-how to exploit it. A strategy can succeed only if it has the backing of the right set of people and other resources. So ask yourself these questions:

- What are our competencies as an organization? How do these give us an advantage relative to competitors?

- What resources support or constrain our actions?

STEP 3: CONSIDER STRATEGIES FOR ADDRESSING THREATS AND OPPORTUNITIES. Clay Christensen has recommended that strategists first prioritize the threats and opportunities they find (he calls them "driving forces" of competition) and then discuss each in broad strokes. If you follow this advice and develop strategies to deal with them, be sure to do the following:

- Create many alternatives. There is seldom only one way to do things. In some cases, the best parts of two strategies can be combined to make a stronger third strategy.

- Check all facts, and question all assumptions.

- Some information is bound to be missing. Determine what information you need to better assess a particular strategy. Then get the information.

- Vet the leading strategy choices among the wisest heads you know. Doing so will help you avoid groupthink within your team.

STEP 4: BUILD A GOOD FIT AMONG STRATEGY-SUPPORTING ACTIVITIES. Michael Porter has made the point that strategy is more than just a blueprint for winning customers; it is also about *combining* activities into a chain whose links are mutually supporting and effective in locking out imitators.[7] He uses Southwest Airlines to illustrate his notion of fit.

Southwest's strategy is based on rapid gate turnaround. Rapid turnaround allows SWA to make frequent departures and better utilize its expensive aircraft assets. This, in turn, supports the low-cost, high-convenience proposition it offers customers. Thus, each of these activities supports the others and the higher goal. That goal, Porter points out, is further supported by other critical activities, which include highly motivated and effective gate personnel and ground crews, a no-meals policy, and a practice of not making interline baggage transfers. Those activities make rapid turnarounds possible. "Southwest's strategy," writes Porter, "involves a whole system of activities, not a collection of parts. Its competitive advantage comes from the way its activities fit and reinforce one another."[8]

STEP 5: CREATE ALIGNMENT. After you've developed a satisfactory strategy, your job is only half finished. The other half is to create alignment between the people and activities of the company and its strategy. Alignment is a condition in which every employee at every level (1) understands the strategy and (2) understands his or her role in making the strategy work. Alignment is a powerful thing. Make sure that you have it working in your favor.

→ great ex. -Disney!

Alignment also involves other resources. Marketing must be focused on the right customers—the ones defined in the strategy. Compensation and bonuses must be aligned with behaviors and performance that advance the strategy. And physical assets must be deployed—aligned—with the highest goals of the organization.

STEP 6: BE PREPARED TO IMPLEMENT. A powerful strategy is impotent if your organization isn't prepared to implement it effectively. Unfortunately, some people get so carried away with the details of their strategy that they forget about the downstream activities required to make it work. One of the benefits of an entrepreneurial start-up is that you're beginning with a clean slate. After you have a strategy, you have a free hand in organizing around it: hiring people with the necessary competencies, acquiring the right equipment, structuring these resources, and so forth. As UCLA's Alfred E. Osborne Jr. has put it, "I think of the 4 S's: structure follows strategy, and staffing follows structure, and you hold the strategy together with systems."[9]

Be Prepared for Change

The initial strategies of start-up companies often fail to hit the mark. Customers don't value the differentiation—or they don't respond to it as anticipated. Or the company is mistaken in its choice of target customers. These failures happen because every start-up business is an experiment to some degree. The outcome of this experiment can surprise and disappoint even the best planners. For example, Webvan's founders and investors thought that a Web-based grocery delivery business was a perfect idea for affluent, Web-savvy, time-starved households. But those customers balked at the higher price of buying their weekly groceries. To them, the extra convenience wasn't worth it.

The entrepreneur's antidote to a disappointing strategy is a willingness to (1) recognize the bad news and (2) respond quickly with a revised strategy. Recognition requires the ability to admit a mistake. Responding requires an energetic search for what went wrong and the flexibility to make adjustments and get back into the game.

Fred's Strategy for The Hybrid Auto Care Center

Strategy is about being different and choosing a different set of activities to deliver a unique mix of value to customers. Let's consider our hypothetical friend Fred and the strategy of his auto repair and maintenance facility.

Fred has clearly differentiated his business. Every town and every city has many automotive service businesses, but one that specializes in hybrid engine vehicles will be very different. Fred can use that distinctiveness to gain customer attention and recognition. You can almost hear the advertising: "If your hybrid car needs maintenance or repair, bring it to the specialists at The Hybrid Auto Care Center. They will do the job right and usually at lower cost than your dealer."

Fred must also deliver on that offer of greater know-how and high-quality work. To do that, Fred must acquire the right resources and align them in support of his distinctive offer. For example, he must hire or train mechanics who really know how to deal with the unique problems of hybrid cars. He must also acquire the tools and diagnostic equipment required by those vehicles.

Successful entrepreneurs are adept at both of these things. They are also masters of incrementalism—that is, if they find that something is working, they do more of it. If they achieve success in a small, niche market, they use what they have and what they have learned to enter another niche—altering the product or service as necessary.

Phase 5 Move to Denver.

A powerful business model and a sound strategy are essential if your venture aims to be competitive and profitable. Although the market provides the ultimate test for these two important concepts, you should test and verify every one of your assumptions before the business is launched. And remember that many minds are better than one. Explain your business model and strategy to as many trusted and experienced people as possible. They may spot defects or opportunities for improvement that you have missed.

Summing Up

- A business model describes an enterprise's revenue sources, cost drivers, investment size, and success factors.

- Strategy differentiates the enterprise and gives it a competitive advantage.

- Per Michael Porter, strategic positions can be found in variety-based, need-based, or access-based positioning.

- The five steps of strategy formulation are (1) looking outside the enterprise for threats and opportunities, (2) looking inside at resources, capabilities, and practices, (3) considering strategies for addressing threats and opportunities, (4) building a good fit among strategy-supporting activities, and (5) creating alignment between the organization's people and activities and its strategy.

- A start-up business should be viewed as an experiment. If the experiment fails to produce the desired result, be prepared to change—and quickly.

Writing a Business Plan

The Basics

Key Topics Covered in This Chapter

- *why you need a business plan*

- *a format that tells readers what they want to know*

- *the importance of the executive summary*

- *how to handle each section of the plan*

- *style features that will make your message stand out*

ABUSINESS PLAN IS a document that explains a business opportunity, identifies the market to be served, and provides details about how the entrepreneurial organization plans to pursue it. Ideally, the business plan describes the unique qualifications that the management team brings to the effort, explains the resources required for success, and provides a forecast of results over a reasonable time horizon.

Every entrepreneur is encouraged to write a business plan, and most take that good advice; those who don't quickly learn that obtaining outside funding is almost impossible without it. Lenders and investors want to see a logical and coherent plan before putting their money at risk. Who wouldn't?

Few entrepreneurs, unfortunately, are skilled at creating a written document that simultaneously (1) makes the best case for the venture, (2) avoids burying the exciting opportunity under a mountain of data, (3) is engaging to read, and (4) gives prospective financiers the information they need to make a decision.

There are plenty of business plan services available, both in major cities and online, that can help you develop a document. For $1,200 and up, these consultants will take your information and work with you to produce a complete, eye-catching plan. There is also plenty of do-it-yourself software available for the business plan writer. These plans, however, are only as good as the ideas and forecasts you put into them. They are no substitute for the substantial thinking on which good plans are based, and that is why some experts suggest that the entrepreneur take control of the entire job.

This short chapter cannot impart all the information you need to write an investment-winning plan, nor can it offer details of what every plan section should contain. You'll find those details in the books and articles mentioned in the "For Further Reading" section of this volume. This chapter aims to impart the serious purposes of a business plan and explain the key points that readers look for in the many plans that cross their desks. If you are not a skillful writer, the final section on style will help you get those points across.

The Purposes of a Business Plan

Ask any entrepreneur why he or she needs a good business plan and you are likely to receive this answer: "You can't get funding without one." This is true, and it explains why many books, advisory services, software, and even M.B.A. courses have been developed to help people write bulletproof, knock-'em-dead business plans. Many leading M.B.A. programs and venture capitalists even sponsor contests that offer funding to whoever writes the most compelling plan. The best and brightest students flock to these contests, hoping to leave campus with a degree *and* financial backing for a start-up company.

Yes, a solid business plan is essential for any business that seeks outside funding from banks, "angels," venture capitalists—even relatives. Absent a good plan, creditors and investors won't take you seriously. They will conclude (perhaps correctly) that you haven't identified your customers or figured out how you will deal profitably with them. The most tolerant funders will say, "Come back and see us when you've put together a complete business plan." The less tolerant will not give your business a second look.

But seeking funding is not the only reason to develop a solid plan. There are several others:

- The act of writing the plan will force you and your team to think through all key elements of your business.

- Trusted and experienced outsiders who review your initial plan will help you identify weaknesses, missed opportunities, unsupportable assumptions, and overly optimistic projections. Finding and fixing these problems on paper will improve your prospects with funders and will reduce the chance of future operational failure.

- A solid plan can be a blueprint for operating your business over the first one or two years, increasing the likelihood of success. The plan will tell you how much you can afford for personnel, advertising, and other expenses. It will specify target customers and success factors.

- The plan's financial projections can be used as a budget. Actual results that fall short of planned results will prompt you to investigate and take corrective action.

These various purposes for the business plan suggest that you tailor plans for different purposes. The intended audience should determine how the plan is written and presented.

Suggested Format

Many venture capital firms review more than a thousand business plans every year—and fund only a few. This means that they don't have time to figure out what you're trying to say. Nor do they have time to deal with people who haven't given them the information they need. The same is true of banks and angel investors. Assuming that you have a worthy idea, you will improve the odds of success if you can grab the reader's attention and keep it. To do this, you must address readers' concerns in a well-organized way.

Figure 5-1 contains a prototype format for a company we will call Lo-Carbo Foods Company, a manufacturer of packaged breakfast and snack foods having low carbohydrate levels. It aims to capitalize on the growing popularity in North America and Europe of low-carb diets. The company's research estimates that twenty-nine million Americans and eight million Europeans are now following low-carb diets, which U.S. government studies have confirmed to be effective in weight reduction and weight control.

FIGURE 5-1

Prototype Business Plan Format

Lo-Carbo Incorporated Business Plan

There is nothing sacred about the format shown here. In fact, you would be wise to tailor your plan format to the likely interests of your readers, just as you would customize the résumé you develop when seeking employment. Thus, you should follow the first rule of every form of writing: Know your audience. The goal in every case is to give readers the information they need to make a decision. (For another format and tips on plan writing, see the CIT/SBA tutorial at www.smallbizlending.com/resources/workshop/sba.htm, or consult the appropriate publications cited in the "For Further Reading" section of this book.)

Let's consider each major section of this document in greater detail.

Contents and Executive Summary

The Contents section (or table of contents) makes it easy for readers to see at a glance what the plan has to offer and where it can be located.

The contents should be followed by an *executive summary*, a short section of two to three pages. In terms of selling your plan to financial backers, this is the most important part of the entire document, so take the time to get it right. The executive summary is not a preface or an introduction; instead, it is a snapshot of the entire plan, something that explains your business to an intelligent reader in only a few minutes. A well-written executive summary captures the interest and attention of readers and prepares them for what follows.

The Opportunity

There is no point in starting or expanding a business unless the entrepreneur has identified a lucrative opportunity. Use this section to describe that opportunity: the market factors driving it, its current size, and its projected size in the years ahead. The point is to get readers to see and appreciate the business opportunity you have identified. So describe the opportunity in terms that are clear and compelling.

For the Lo-Carbo Foods Company, for example, you would use this section to describe the latest findings about rampant obesity in the United States and signs of the same in Western Europe. You would point to research estimating that twenty-nine million Americans and eight million Europeans are now following low-carb diets, and you would cite independent scientific studies that confirm the effectiveness of low-carbohydrate diets. An overview of consumer spending on health foods and weight control foods might also be provided here.

Use this section also to highlight the economics underlying the opportunity and the factors that will drive its success, such as market penetration, product innovation, and so on. But don't get carried away. Keep it brief, focused, and upbeat.

This is also a suitable place to cite the magnitude of the funding being sought and to explain how it will be used in pursuing the opportunity. For example, the Lo-Carbo plan might include something like this:

Lo-Carbo is seeking $2.75 million in funding to pursue this opportunity. The bulk of those funds will be used to exploit its current success

*and growing interest in the company's existing products by a national
vendor of high-protein/low-carbohydrate foods.*

Although it is important to document the opportunity with objective data, don't turn this section into a boring "data dump." Don't
allow your compelling story to be buried under a mountain of facts.
Instead, summarize the data and explain its implications for investors. Put the actual documentation in an appendix.

The Company, Its Products (or Services), and Strategy

Use this section to describe the company, explain how it is organized, and state its essential purpose. Here is an example: *the Company.*

*Lo-Carbo is a Colorado-based corporation. It was founded in 2001
with the goal of serving a growing interest in a high-protein and low-
carbohydrate diet. Its experienced management team has developed and
test-marketed several low-carbohydrate products, primarily breakfast and
snack foods. These products are not merely low in carbohydrates; tests
have confirmed that they are also tasty and satisfying—qualities that
differentiate them from other low-carb foods. The products are as follows:* Product

- *Mellow Morning, a whole wheat and barley breakfast cereal with
  48 percent fewer carbohydrates than leading conventional breakfast
  cereals. Mellow Morning meets the specifications of the leading low-
  carb diets.*

- *Crackle Brackle, a crisped, steel-cut oatmeal product for breakfast
  eating and for baking. Like Mellow Morning, Crackle Brackle meets
  the specifications of leading low-carb diets.*

- *Compadre Lo-Carb Chips, the company's tortilla chip. It too meets
  low-carb diet requirements while being flavorful and satisfying.*

  *Each of these products was well received in market tests (see the
  Appendix for details) and is currently being sold through two regional
  health food stores: Nutrimarket Stores, Inc., and Pleasant Valley Farms,
  Inc. Other products are in development.*

GOALS. Don't forget to include a subsection about the goals of the company and its business strategy. Investors will want to know how you plan to grow. If there is a chance that the company will become a tempting acquisition target for a larger, less innovative competitor, mention this possibility. Here is an example:

Lo-Carbo has three goals:

1. To broaden its product line

2. To expand market penetration through stores and through a private labeling agreement with one of the major diet companies (currently in negotiations)

3. To expand the business to the point where it either becomes a dominant player in the low-carbohydrate food niche or is acquired by one of the packaged food industry giants. In this industry, small companies with one or two successful products are often bought out at premium prices.

If your company's products are not yet market-ready, you should reveal your plans for product rollouts. Also include an artist's rendering of the final physical product. If your products are market-ready, go beyond the written description; include high-quality photographs.

YOUR STRATEGY. Include in this or a separate section a discussion of the company's strategy. Strategy is about differentiation and competitive advantage. Explain what is different about your company's approach to the marketplace and how that difference will give it a sustainable competitive advantage. Differentiation may reside in the product or service—for example, a technically superior semiconductor that provides greater value to customers. On the other hand, differentiation may reside in your approach to customers, as in Dell's initial decision to sell custom-configured personal computers directly to users, bypassing the retail channel.

What makes your product or service, or means of delivery, different—and more desirable—in the eyes of customers? How will that difference translate into a competitive advantage that will produce profits and growing equity value? Investors want clear answers to these questions. Spell them out here.

OWNERSHIP. This "Company" section is also a fitting location for ownership information:

- Who are the current owners, and what percentages do they control?

- How is ownership evidenced—for example, in terms of common and preferred stock?

- Have any options, warrants, or convertible bonds that could expand ownership been issued?

- Which owners are involved in the day-to-day workings of the business?

The Management Team

Investors are keen to know about the people behind the business, whom they see as key assets. Specifically, what experiences or qual-

About Intellectual Property

Is your competitive advantage based on a proprietary technology or process? Is that technology or process patented or "patentable"? Does the company own patents, copyrights, or valuable trademarks? If it does, when will they expire?

Many businesses are formed around one or another piece of intellectual property. Some are key assets that impact competitive advantage over a period of time. Readers of your plan will want to know what steps you've taken to protect that property and to keep technical and market know-how within the organization, where it will produce revenues and profits for investors.

ifications do they bring to the enterprise? "When I receive a business plan," writes professor-practitioner Bill Sahlman, "I always read the résumé section first. Not because the people part of the new venture is the most important, but because without the right team, none of the other parts really matter."[1]

Fourteen Personnel Questions Every Business Plan Should Answer

- Where are the founders from?

- Where have they been educated?

- Where have they worked—and for whom?

- What have they accomplished—professionally and person-ally—in the past?

- What is their reputation within the business community?

- What experience do they have that is directly relevant to the opportunity they are pursuing?

- What skills, abilities, and knowledge do they have?

- How realistic are they about the venture's chances for success and the tribulations it will face?

- Who else needs to be on the team?

- Are they prepared to recruit high-quality people?

- How will they respond to adversity?

- Do they have the mettle to make the inevitable hard choices that must be made?

- How committed are they to this venture?

- What are their motivations?

SOURCE: William A. Sahlman, "How to Write a Great Business Plan," *Harvard Business Review*, July–August 1997, 101. Used with permission.

Here's how Lo-Carbo's business plan describes its people:

The management team is made up of Joanne Galloway, Dr. Philip Lindstrom, Gunter Schwartz, and Carlos Talavera. Together, they bring exceptional technical expertise and business experience to the enterprise.

- *Joanne Galloway has fifteen years of product and general management experience with packaged food companies, most recently with Gigantic Foods Corporation.*

- *Philip Lindstrom has a Ph.D. in nutrition. He joined the company in 2002 after working for ten years in product development for Behemoth Foods.*

- *Gunther Schwartz, the team's manufacturing expert, has been in the processed foods business for twelve years with both Behemoth Foods and Food Science Laboratories, a contract food research organization. Among Mr. Schwartz's accomplishments is the extrusion process used to manufacture Snackarinos and Caloritos, two highly successful packaged snack brands owned by Behemoth Foods.*

- *Carlos Talavera left his position as vice president of marketing at Healthtone, a leading packaged foods company, to join Galloway and Lindstrom in founding Lo-Carbo.*

Note: Complete résumés can be found in the appendix.

Most plans use an organization chart to indicate the reporting relationships among key personnel. A table indicating names, titles, and salaries is also useful, as in table 5-1.

Assuming that your company is a corporation, this is also an appropriate place to identify the board of directors. You should indicate the names of board members, their positions on the board, their professional backgrounds, and their history of involvement with the company.

Marketing Plan

If the "people" section of your business plan gets the most attention from readers, the marketing plan runs a close second. Investors know

TABLE 5-1

Lo-Carbo Inc., Key Personnel

	Position	Salary
Joanne Galloway	CEO	$85,000
Philip Lindstrom	VP Product Development	$75,000
Gunther Schwartz	VP Manufacturing	$75,000
Carlos Talavera	VP Sales & Marketing	$75,000
Edward Johnson	Financial consultant	Day rate
Diane Wolfe	Adminstrative assistant	$40,000

that marketing is the activity most associated with success or failure. An attractive product or service is essential, but a company will fail if it cannot connect with customers. A sound and realistic marketing plan is the best assurance that a solid customer connection will be made. The plan should be clear about all aspects of marketing, including the following:

- Identification of customers

- The number of potential customers and potential sales revenues

- The requirements of various customer segments

- The importance of purchase convenience, rapid delivery, product customization, and so on for these segments

- Ways to effectively access each segment—through distributors, a captive sales force, direct mail, e-commerce, or whatever

- Appropriate sales and promotion approaches

- An analysis of how purchase decisions are made

- Customer price sensitivity

- The cost of acquiring and retaining customers

- The strengths and weaknesses of competitors and ways that competitors are likely to react when the company enters the market

The Board of Directors

Every corporation must, by law, have a board of directors. But the entrepreneur should go beyond the requirements of the law in enlisting members. A board shouldn't be just a bunch of warm bodies. Instead, it should be an effective sounding board for ideas and a source of sage advice.

Recruiting board members should be a matter of the highest importance. You want people who have abundant business experience and, if technology is essential to the business, considerable scientific or engineering know-how. Board members should also be respected in the broader business community. Their capabilities and integrity will speak volumes to whoever reads your business plan, financiers in particular.

For your plan to be credible, these issues should be supported with solid market intelligence. Summarize that supporting intelligence here, and refer readers to whatever market research you've provided in the appendix.

Operating Plan

Whether you're in the business of designing products, manufacturing them, acting as a distributor, or running an e-commerce site, you are faced with a host of operational issues. What supplier relationships do you have or envision? How much inventory will be required? If you are a manufacturer, will you follow a job shop or continuous flow operation? Which day-to-day operating chores will be handled internally, and which will be outsourced?

An operations plan considers the many details of converting inputs to outputs that customers value. What is your plan?

Financial Plan

If a company is already operating, it will have (or should have) a set of financial statements: a *balance sheet*, an *income statement*, and a *cash flow statement.*[2] In a nutshell, the balance sheet describes what the company owns—its assets—and how those assets have been financed (through liabilities and the funds of the current owners) as of a particular date.

The income statement reveals the company's revenues, what it spent to gain those revenues, and the interest and taxes it paid over a specified period. Finally, the cash flow statement tells readers the sources and uses of cash during the same period. Together, these three financial statements reveal much to the trained eye of potential investors. (Note: If you are not familiar with these statements, see appendix A for an explanation of the basics.)

Generally, it's best to place the full financial statements in the appendix to your business plan. Use this space for key data from those statements—data that will give readers the big picture of your business and its intended future. Key among these data are your sales and expense projections, described earlier in this book as a pro forma income statement. For a company such as Lo-Carbo, readers would be interested in a breakout of key items in the statement, such as the anticipated revenues from various channels of distribution, as shown in table 5–2. Here we see anticipated sales and sales growth by channel and the percentage of sales represented by each.

TABLE 5-2

**Forecast Revenues by Distribution Channel
(in $000 and % of Sales)**

	2005	%	2006	%	2007	%
Net sales						
Health food stores	112	100	160	80	200	38
Supermarkets	0	0	40	20	80	15
Private label business	0	0	0	0	240	46
Total Sales	112	100	200	100	520	99

TABLE 5-3

Forecast Marketing Expenses (in $000 and % of Sales)

	2005	%	2006	%	2007	%
Marketing expenses						
Sales commissions	11	*10*	20	*9*	52	*9*
Research	70	*63*	80	*36*	85	*15*
Promotion	20	*18*	32	*15*	50	*9*
Total expense	101	*91*	132	*60*	187	*33*

Consider doing the same for key categories of operating expenses, such as marketing cost, as shown in table 5-3.

Naturally, sales projections and other items in these pro forma statements are based on assumptions. Experienced investors are keenly aware of this and will want to know what those assumptions are and why you made them. Make that part of your discussion.

Style

Every business plan is a combination of style and substance. Not being wordsmiths, most entrepreneurs concentrate on the substance and shortchange the style. That's unfortunate, because inattention to style makes a plan dull and difficult to read.

One remedy is to work with a writer who has experience in business plan writing. Another is to be your own wordsmith and observe the rules of good writing: Use words sparingly, keep sentences simple, make the most of design elements, and use graphics judiciously.

Visualizing the Bottom Line

Some people learn best from written material. Others are more receptive to the spoken word. Still others—and that includes most of us—learn from pictures and graphic representations of numerical data. So it's a good idea to use graphics to summarize your financial data.

Harvard professor Bill Sahlman suggests a "time to positive cash flow" graph like the one shown here. This image helps the investor see at a glance the expected depth and duration of negative cash flow, as well as the relationship between the investment and the potential return. "The ideal, needless to say," says Sahlman, "is to have cash flow early and often. But most investors are intrigued by the picture even when the cash outflow is high and long—as long as the cash inflow is more so."

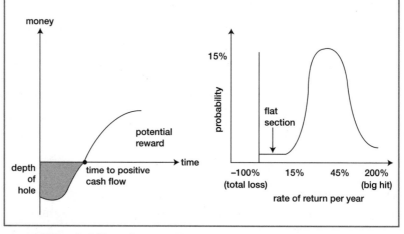

SOURCE: William A. Sahlman, "How to Write a Great Business Plan," *Harvard Business Review,* July–August 1997, 104.

Use Words Sparingly

In the business world, shorter is always better if it communicates the required information. So heed Rule 17 in Strunk and White's timeless *Elements of Style*, and omit needless words.

> *Vigorous writing is concise. A sentence should contain no unnecessary words; a paragraph no unnecessary sentences; for the same reason that a drawing should have no unnecessary lines and a machine no unnecessary parts. This requires not that the writer make all his sentences short, or that he avoid all detail and treat his subjects only in outline, but that every word tells.*[3]

This quote from Strunk and White is itself a perfect model of their rule. They use no unnecessary words; every word makes a contribution. Economy of words has two big benefits for the business plan writer: Your key messages will stand out, and economy of words saves your reader's valuable time.

Use Simple Sentences

The sentence is the basic unit of written expression. Most sentences make a statement. The statement can be simple or complex. Consider these:

1. The growing popularity of low-carbohydrate diets has created a business opportunity for makers of low-carb foods.

2. On the one hand we witness rising levels of obesity among children and adults, both in North America and in Western Europe, which in turn have increased the popularity of low-carb diets, which in turn have created a business opportunity for Lo-Carb Company and other makers of low-carb foods.

The first sentence, unlike the second, is spare and to the point. It will more likely register with readers. It does not contain all the information found in the second. If that information is important, it should be provided in a separate sentence.

Packing more information into each sentence is not necessarily bad, nor does it violate rules of grammar if done properly. However, complex sentences make the reader work harder and may create confusion. As a writer, your challenge is to know when a sentence has reached its optimal carrying capacity.

Use Design Elements to Lighten the Reader's Load

Readers of your business plan are busy people who have learned to skim; they drill down only to relevant details. You can facilitate their skimming through the use of design elements. Design elements include headings, subheads, and short blocks of text. Even white space can be used as a design element. All are useful in long documents. Used judiciously, they can

- make your written documents more inviting to the reader

- improve reader comprehension

- help speed the reader through your material

USE HEADINGS AND SUBHEADS. Headings and subheads signal that a new or related topic is about to begin. They give your work greater eye appeal and "skimmability." You can also use headings and subheads to impart key ideas. For example, our heading "Use Headings and Subheads" is also a key idea. A time-constrained reader can gather the key points of any section in your business plan by simply reading these headings and subheads.

BREAK UP LONG BLOCKS OF TEXT. Long, uninterrupted blocks of text are off-putting to readers and are difficult to skim. Headings and subheads can help you break those blocks into identifiable small bites. So can short paragraphs. Some experts recommend that paragraphs average no more than two hundred words—about five sentences, or 1.5 inches of single-spaced typing.

Numbered lists are another effective way to break up long, intimidating blocks of text and to increase the impact. You can use numbered lists to summarize key points or to get your ideas across quickly, as in the following example:

Our study of the market for low-carb foods uncovered four primary channels for reaching end-use customers:

1. Health food retail stores (currently 34,000 in the U.S. alone)

2. Stand-alone low-carb food stores (currently only 43, but growing quickly in numbers)

3. Traditional grocery stores (health food section)

4. Private labeling of products sold through one or more of the low-carb diet plans

Notice how the numbered list breaks up the page and gets conclusions across in a way that they cannot be missed.

Bullets can serve the same purposes as numbered lists. Bullets are sometimes the best way to get information across clearly and succinctly—if not elegantly. For example, you might use a bulleted list when you

• want to highlight a sequence of actions

• need to organize a list of items

• need to list parts of a whole

Bullets (or numbers) are not needed when your list has only one or two elements. In these cases you can usually get by saying something like this:

Focus groups identified two problems with our competitor's low-carb tortilla chips: They taste like cardboard and cause gastric distress.

Let Graphics Tell Part of the Story

Business plans inevitably contain lots of numerical data. When it comes to transmitting numerical data quickly, bar charts and pie charts are hard to beat. Readers can see at a glance what they would otherwise have to extract from many tedious lines of verbiage and numbers. Which of the following would you rather read? Which of the following would make a more memorable impression?

Text-only example:

Our survey found that 2 percent of the people who come downtown in a typical day do so by bicycle. Some 9 percent arrive by public transportation. Thirty-five percent respond that they walk to the downtown, while the largest single group—54 percent—arrive by automobile.

Text and graphics example (see figure 5-2):

According to our survey, people arrive downtown by various means, most by automobile.

A Caution on Design Elements

Don't get carried away with design elements. Word processing software gives you an arsenal of design features: boldface, italics, dozens of font sizes and styles, clip art, chart-making tools, and so forth. Used judiciously, these add to the appearance and readability of your text. Overuse them, however, and you will create the opposite effect and make your work appear amateurish. So keep it simple.

There is no general rule about the appropriateness and inappropriateness of design features. Every piece is unique. When in doubt, obtain a professionally produced business plan of another company and use it as a model.

FIGURE 5-2

How People Reach the Downtown

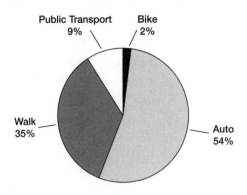

Notice that telling the story with a graphic doesn't necessarily save space, but it gives your audience a break from reading text, and it generally has more impact.

Final Thoughts

As you develop your business plan, always keep the interests of your readers in mind. Put yourself in their place. Your audience is looking for convincing evidence that you have found a real business opportunity—one with substantial growth possibilities. Considering the risks they will be taking with their money, they want to see major upside potential.

Your plan's readers will also be looking for clear indications that you have done your homework—that you understand the market, have targeted the right customers, and have developed a sound strategy for profitably transacting business with them. Prospective investors want assurance that you and the management team have the knowledge, experience, and drive to turn an opportunity into a profitable business. And what is important to potential lenders and

---

The Software Solution

Business plan software programs are available for $200 or less. Business PlanPro is one example. Some matchmaker firms even offer downloadable templates that provide the basic structure of the plan and ask you to "fill in the blanks" for the component parts, including cash flow and sales projections. For software and templates, search the Internet using "business plan" and "business plan software" as keywords.

---

investors should be just as important to you. So as you write your plan, stop periodically and ask yourself, Is this a real opportunity? Do I understand the market and the customers I hope to attract? Can we really make this thing work?

Finally, tell your readers how they will get their money out of the company.

Investors want an exit strategy: a buyout by management, an acquisition by another company, an initial public offering of shares, and so on. Even if you plan to be in the business for the long haul, your investors want liquidity at some point—and the sooner the better.

Summing Up

- Keep the audience foremost in your mind as you develop your business plan.

- Your business plan should tell readers in a compelling way everything they need to know to make a decision.

- Although the principal reason for writing a business plan is to obtain outside funding, the act of writing it will force the management team to think through all key elements of the business.

- The executive summary should, in compelling terms, explain the opportunity, tell why it is timely, show how your company plans to pursue it, describe your expected results, and provide a thumbnail sketch of the company and the management team.

- Among other things, the plan should state the company's goals and explain how investors will eventually cash out.

- Pay attention to style. Use as few words as necessary to get your points across. Avoid long, complex sentences when possible. Make your document easy to skim by using headings, sub-heads, white space, and numbered and bulleted lists to break up blocks of text.

6

Financing the Business

Where's the Money?

Key Topics Covered in This Chapter

- *a life-cycle overview*

- *start-up financing*

- *financing current operations*

- *financing growth*

- *proper matching of assets and financing*

- *typical financing arrangements*

MONEY GREASES THE wheels of enterprise. Without it, even the boldest and best business plan would remain nothing more than a document. Money is an essential ingredient of enterprise at every level—for the corner bookstore and for the national bookstore chain with four hundred retail outlets. It is needed at every stage of business development: at the launch and again when the start-up forges through various levels of growth. Even a mature business with annual sales in the billions of dollars needs continued financing to stay on the cutting edge of its field.

This chapter describes the financing requirements that businesses typically encounter in the phases of the business life cycle, from start-up to maturity. It also provides an overview of the sources they turn to in securing financing during those phases. Two types of business—lifestyle and entrepreneurial—are used to illustrate the general course of financing from start-up through expansion.

A Life–Cycle View of Financing

It is useful to stand back and observe the theoretical life cycle of business inception, growth, and maturity. Doing so helps us understand how and when various forms of financing—and various financing institutions—come into play.

The Lifestyle Enterprise

The easiest business life cycle to understand is the one associated with the lifestyle enterprise—the business whose goal is to provide income and a retirement nest egg for the founder and his or her family. This type of business has a start-up phase, followed perhaps by a period of gradual growth, followed by a no-growth phase of maturity. The owner requires start-up financing to purchase or lease equipment, rent a workplace, establish an inventory and fixtures, and provide working capital. In many cases, the entrepreneur is simply purchasing an existing lifestyle business from someone else.

What are the sources of financing for this type of business? Typically they are *BOOTSTRAP FINANCING:*

- personal savings

- credit card lines of credit

- a second mortgage on the founder's home

- loans from friends and relatives

- short-term trade credit from suppliers

Many refer to this type of start-up financing as bootstrap financing. There is no big money involved. Bootstrap financing is the rule rather than the exception, even among successful companies, according to research conducted by Amar Bhidé, a business school professor and former McKinsey consultant. Bhidé and his associates interviewed the founders of one hundred companies on the 1989 *Inc. Magazine* 500 list of the fastest-growing private U.S. companies. Bhidé found that more than 80 percent were initially financed through the founders' personal resources (as in the foregoing list), including one that used a $50 personal check—a check that bounced. The median amount of start-up capital used by these companies was about $10,000 (in late 1980s U.S. dollars).[1]

To better appreciate the challenge of start-up financing and the available sources of funds, consider the case of a fictitious company.

When Angus McDuff started a woodworking business in 1963, he was well prepared for self-employment. His transition from being a supervisor at a small wooden lamp-making concern to proprietor of his own business was direct. As a supervisor, he knew all about shaping and fitting lumber into commercial products. He knew the material suppliers on a first-name basis, and he was often in contact with wholesale and retail distributors of his company's finished products.

McDuff had used the final year of his employment productively. In his spare time, he designed a small line of wooden hat racks, used his experience in the lamp business to calculate his production costs, and learned a great deal about the channels of distribution through which his new products would be sold. So when he walked away from his job and became a business owner, he was extremely well prepared.

Starting the venture, however, required more than knowledge. Financial and production assets were also required. McDuff calculated that he would need enough cash—say, $3,000—to tide him over a three-month start-up period in which he was bound to generate and collect little sales revenue. He'd also need an inventory of lumber, hardware fixtures, and other materials. Those items of material inventory would be transformed into finished-goods inventory over time. And he'd also need money to pay for an annual property and liability insurance policy and the first three months of rent on a small workshop. He calculated that he'd need $7,300 for these assets, as shown in table 6-1.

McDuff's business, which he decided to call Amalgamated Hat Rack Company, also needed some fixed assets: a wood lathe, a few power and hand tools, workbenches for the shop, and a panel truck for picking up materials and making customer deliveries. Fortunately, Angus's employer offered to sell him an old panel truck and many of the required tools, two used wood lathes, and several surplus workbenches for a total price of $3,000.

With these, Angus was able to complete the fixed-asset section of his balance sheet (table 6-2). When added to his current asset requirements, he figured that he'd need assets totaling $10,300 to launch his venture.

McDuff's requirement of $10,300 in assets might not seem like much, but remember that this was 1963, when a dollar was actually

TABLE 6-1

Current Asset Requirements

Cash		$3,000
Inventory		
Lumber	$800	
Hardware	$700	
Other	$500	
Total inventory		$2,000
Prepaid expenses		
Insurance (1 year)	$800	
Rent (3 months)	$1,500	
Total prepaid expenses		$2,300
Total current assets		$7,300

TABLE 6-2

Fixed-Asset Requirements

Used panel truck	$1,200	
Lathes	$1,200	
Other tools	$300	
Shop fixtures	$300	
Total fixed assets		$3,000
Total current assets (from table 6-1)		$7,300
Total current and fixed assets		$10,300

worth something! So how was he going to finance these modest start-up costs? Fortunately, Angus and his wife, Alice, had $5,300 available in their savings account, and Alice's uncle offered to contribute the rest in the form of a zero-interest loan of $5,000. "You can pay me back at $1,000 per year," he told them. "And good luck with the business." Altogether, they had the financing they needed to get the business rolling.

And that's how Amalgamated was initially financed. You've already seen the asset side of the balance sheet. Table 6-3 is the liabilities and owners' equity side, which spells out how the company's assets were financed.

TABLE 6-3

Liabilities and Owners' Equity

Current liabilities (current portion of five-year loan)	$1,000
Long-term liabilities (balance of five-year loan)	$4,000
Total liabilities	$5,000
Owners' equity	$5,300
Total liabilities and owners' equity	$10,300

Many, if not most, small businesses are initially financed in a manner similar to the Amalgamated case—with the owner-operator's personal savings and with contributions from friends and family members. Some individuals even resort to using their credit card lines of credit for start-up capital, expensive as that is.

Trade Credit

Many small-business owners obtain thirty- to sixty-day trade credit from their suppliers as one component of their start-up (and ongoing) financing. For example, a shoe-store owner may be able to obtain $3,000 worth of shoes from a wholesaler, with payment due in sixty days. By having picked inventory wisely, the owner may be able to sell all or most of the shoes during that sixty-day period and use the proceeds to pay the wholesaler's bill in full when it comes due. In effect, the supplier will have financed the store's inventory without charge—a better deal for the owner than using a bank line of credit or another device that involves interest charges.

Commercial Bank Loans

Some start-ups may also find limited financing from commercial banks. Banks are usually reluctant to offer long-term loans to small firms. They are more eager to extend short-term demand loans, seasonal lines of credit, and single-purpose loans for machinery and equipment. Bankers are justifiably nervous about making long-term or unsecured loans to start-up businesses, because the failure rate is high. Most local banks will extend loans to a start-up only if they are comfortable with the situation and the qualifications of the borrower.

What makes bank lenders comfortable? Bankers ask three questions before they lend money, and they rarely part with their capital if they cannot obtain satisfactory answers to all three:

1. Will the borrower be able to pay me back?

2. Is the borrower's character such that he or she will pay me back?

3. If the borrower fails to repay me, what marketable assets can I get my hands on?

In seeking an answer to the first question, a banker will evaluate the entrepreneur's skills and the business plan:

- Does the applicant understand the market and have a feasible plan for satisfying it?

- Does the entrepreneur have the experience or knowledge—or both—required to operate this type of business successfully?

- Is the business plan realistic, complete, and based on reasonable assumptions?

- Are the plan's revenue and cost projections realistic and conservative? Because loan repayments will be made from cash flow, a lender will be particularly interested in projected cash flow.

If the business is already operating, the banker will look to the prospective borrower's *current ratio* to get a sense of his or her ability to repay the loan. The current ratio is represented by this simple formula:

Current Ratio = Current Assets / Current Liabilities

Because *current assets* (cash, securities, accounts receivable, inventory) can be turned readily into cash, this ratio imparts a sense of a company's ability to pay its bills (*current liabilities*) as they come due.

The size of the current ratio that a healthy company needs to maintain depends on the relationship between inflows of cash and demands for cash payments. A company that has a continuous and reliable inflow of cash or other liquid assets, such as a public utility or a taxi company, may be able to meet currently maturing obligations easily despite a small current ratio—say, 1.10 (which means that the company has $1.10 in current assets for every $1.00 of current liabilities). On the other hand, a manufacturing firm with a long product development and manufacturing cycle may need to maintain a larger current ratio.

To confirm the absolute liquidity of an organization, a bank credit analyst can modify the current ratio by eliminating from current assets all those that cannot be liquidated on very short notice. Typically then, this ratio, called the *acid-test ratio*, consists of the ratio of so-called quick assets (cash, marketable securities, and accounts receivable) to current liabilities. Inventory is left out of the calculation.

Acid-Test Ratio = Quick Assets / Current Liabilities

Paradoxically, a company can have loads of choice assets—office buildings, fleets of delivery trucks, and warehouses brimming with finished-goods inventory—and still risk insolvency if its ratio of current (or quick) assets is insufficient to meet bills as they come due. Creditors don't take payment in used delivery trucks; they want cash.

Lenders generally answer the second question—"Is the borrower's character such that he or she will pay me back?"—by examining the loan applicant's credit history. Whether it's a car loan, a home mortgage, or a business loan, a banker will seek evidence that the applicant pays bills on schedule.

The third question—"What assets can I get my hands on?"—is about *collateral*. Collateral is an asset pledged to the lender until such time as the loan is satisfied. In an automobile loan, for example, the lender retains title to the vehicle and makes sure that the buyer has made a sufficiently large down payment so that the lender can repossess the car, sell it, and fully reimburse itself from the proceeds if the borrower fails to make timely loan payments.

Business loans are similar. The lender wants to see assets that, in the case of business failure, can be sold to satisfy the loan. Those as-

> ## U.S. Small Business Administration (SBA) Loans
>
> The SBA administers three loan programs intended to help small businesses owned by U.S. citizens obtain financing. SBA does not itself grant loans; rather, it sets guidelines for loans, and its partners (lenders, community development organizations, and microlending institutions) make the loans. What makes these deals palatable to financial institutions is that the SBA guarantees repayment up to certain levels, eliminating some of the lender's risk.
>
> Information about the SBA loan program can be found at www.sba.gov. This same site provides abundant information about starting and managing a small business.

sets might be current assets such as cash, inventory, and accounts receivable; they might also include fixed assets such as vehicles, buildings, and equipment. High-tech start-ups that organize around development of a new technology rarely have assets with collateral value; consequently, bank loans are usually not available to them.

Life–Cycle Financing of the Entrepreneurial Company

Most businesses never grow large and never have the potential for doing so. They may expand over the years to the point of generating $10 million to $20 million in annual revenue, but that's the limit. Angus McDuff's hat rack company may be one of these. Others have much greater potential for growth, even though they too may begin as tiny enterprises. Microsoft was one of these, even though it began with a handful of geeky programmers working out of a motel room, writing code night and day, and subsisting on beer and pizza. The little company started by Steve Jobs and Steve Wozniak in Jobs's garage is another; its Apple II launched the era of the personal computer and propelled the little company to big-company status.

Business scholars call these "entrepreneurial" companies. Their life cycle is shown in figure 6-1. Beyond the start-up phase is a period of growth, followed by a mature phase. Naturally, few entrepreneurial companies make it through all three phases. Many fail within a few years. Still others are acquired by larger corporations before they reach their full potential. Very few make it through the entire cycle to maturity. Those that do may become the Hewlett-Packards, Sonys, Virgin Groups, and Wal-Marts of the corporate world.

FIGURE 6-1

The Entrepreneurial Company Life Cycle

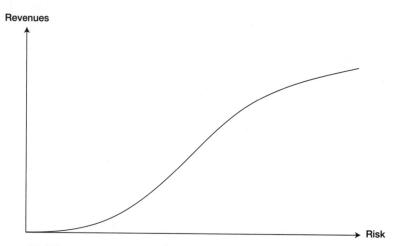

Start-Up	Growth	Maturity
• Personal savings	• Internal cash flow	• Secondary share offering
• Loans from friends, etc.	• Bank loan	• Bond sale
• Credit cards	• Venture capital	• Money center bank loan
• Home equity loan	• IPO	• Commercial paper
• Trade credit from suppliers	• Asset-based loans/leases	• Asset-based loans/leases
• Local angels		

Start-up Phase Financing

The entrepreneurial firm usually finds start-up financing in the same pockets as its lifestyle cousins: the personal savings and credit of the owner, loans or ownership capital provided by friends, relatives, and members of the management team, and perhaps a small bank loan. However, if the founder and the management team have strong reputations in the business or scientific community, they may attract capital from angel investors or even a venture capital firm. This is especially true if the founder has enjoyed past entrepreneurial success. Financiers love people with a demonstrated Midas touch, and they pursue them actively. In these cases, the company may attract investors long before it has a marketable product or service, and certainly before it enters the growth phase.

Growth Phase Financing

During this phase the business expands its sales and develops a growing base of customers. As a result, more capital typically is required—for operational expansion, the hiring and training of new personnel, and even acquisitions. Some of that capital may be generated internally from positive cash flows. But more is needed if growth is strong or if the business's strategy is to build brand visibility. Having proven its credibility as a business operation, the enterprise can generally tap external capital more easily than it could previously.

Debt capital in this phase often comes from local banks. Debt is one of the lowest-cost sources of external capital because interest charges (in the U.S. tax system) are deductible from taxable income. This deductibility, of course, doesn't do a company much good if it has no taxable income to report, a common situation for early-stage companies.

The degree to which the activities of a company are supported by liabilities and long-term debt as opposed to owners' capital contributions is called *leverage*. A firm that has a high proportion of debt relative to owner contributions is said to be highly leveraged. For owners, the advantage of having high debt is that returns on their actual investments can be disproportionately higher when the company makes a profit. On the other hand, high leverage is a negative when cash flows fall, because the interest on debt is a contractual obligation that must be paid in bad times as well as good. A company can be forced into bankruptcy by the crush of interest payments due on its outstanding debt.

The *debt ratio* is widely used to assess the degree of leverage used by companies and its attendant risks. It is calculated in different ways, two of which are illustrated here. The simplest is this:

Debt Ratio = Total Debt / Total Assets

Alternatively, you can calculate the debt-to-equity ratio by dividing the total liabilities by the amount of shareholders' equity:

Debt-to-Equity Ratio = Total Liabilities / Owners' Equity

In general, as either of these ratios increases, the returns to owners are higher, but so too are the risks. Creditors understand this relationship extremely well and often include specific limits on the debt levels beyond which borrowers may not go without having their loans called in.

Creditors also use the *times interest earned ratio* to estimate how safe it is to lend money to individual businesses. The formula for this ratio is:

Times Interest Earned Ratio = Earnings before Interest
and Taxes / Interest Expense

The number of times that interest payments are covered by pretax earnings, or *EBIT* (earnings before interest and taxes), indicates the degree to which income could fall without causing insolvency. In many cases, this is not so much a test of solvency as a test of staying power under adversity. For example, if EBIT were to be cut in half because of a recession or another cause, would the company still have sufficient earnings to meet its interest obligations?

The counterweight to heavy debt is owners' equity. Equity capital is obtained through the sale of shares to investors, including the entrepreneur. The typical entrepreneurial enterprise in the growth phase is neither large enough nor proven enough to become a pub-

About Venture Capitalists

A *venture capitalist* (VC), or a VC firm, is a high-risk investor who seeks an equity position in a start-up or an early-growth company having high potential. In return for capital, the VC typically takes a significant percentage of ownership of the business and a position on its board. VCs are very engaged in the strategic management of their fledgling companies and often are instrumental in connecting them with suppliers and potential business allies. In many cases, VCs help recruit the technical and managerial personnel these companies need to succeed.

Generally, VCs seek out small firms that have the potential to return ten times their risk capital within five years. Most aim to harvest their investments during the initial public offering or follow-on issues of company share and then to move on to the next opportunity. Look for more on venture capitalists later in this book.

lic company—that is, to launch an initial public offering (IPO) of shares. As a result, it cannot tap broader equity markets. If the company is in a "hot" growth industry, or if it is close to producing a breakthrough with some game-changing product, it may gain the attention of a venture capital firm. If this private investor likes the looks of the business, it may make a sizable capital contribution.

Most companies never get beyond the early phase of growth. They either fail or are acquired. But those that succeed have access to a broader spectrum of financing opportunities—in particular, the public stock market. The prospect of even greater growth is a powerful lure to equity investors, who hope to buy shares while shares are still cheap and the company is unrecognized.

Local banks are also important sources of external financing as growth continues. The business now has a confidence-inspiring record of producing revenues and paying its bills. Its current and time interest earned ratios are favorable. And it has assets that it can pledge as collateral for asset-based loans or leases. The company may also have grown so much that it has outgrown the lending capacity of its local bank, in which case it can move upstream to a large money-center bank. Amar Bhidé's study of successful and growing firms on the *Inc.* 500 list indicated that fewer than one-fifth of those firms financed growth through the sale of ownership shares to outsiders during the first five years. Instead, they borrowed money or used internally generated cash to pay for expansion.[2]

The major milestone in the growth phase for those few enterprises that show exceptional promise is the *initial public offering* of stock, or *IPO*. IPOs are managed by one or more investment banking firms selected by the issuing company. The investment bankers help the issuing company navigate through the strict regulatory requirements of issuing shares to the public. More important, the investment bank and its syndicate of broker-dealers (stockbrokers) provide direct access to millions of potential investors: individual investors, mutual funds, pension funds, and private money managers. Subsequent chapters will provide you with more information on investment bankers. Table 6-4 summarizes the pros and cons of various forms of capital sources during the growth phase.

TABLE 6-4

Growth Stage Capital Sources for the Entrepreneurial Company

Internal cash flow from operations	• Cost-free if shareholders eager anxious for dividends. • May not be enough to finance substantial growth in the productive base of the business.
Debt capital	• Costly, but interest payments are deductible from taxable income (if there is any). • Interest rate is a function of prevailing rates, the term of the loan, and the creditworthiness of the borrower. • Debt increases the riskiness of the enterprise.
Venture capital	• The most expensive capital available because the VC will take a significant share of ownership—and of future prospects for the company. • The entrepreneur must share power with the VC. • Unlike any other form of capital, this one comes with business advice that may be valuable.
Initial public offering	• Perhaps the only way to round up a large bundle of money. But like venture capital, it dilutes the ownership interests of the entrepreneur and earlier investors. Also, the duties of being a public company are often onerous.

Maturity Phase Financing

Trees do not grow to the skies. Nor do growth companies continue growing forever. Eventually, growth tapers off for one or more reasons:

- Success and profitability draw competitors into the market.

- Demand for the product or service is largely satisfied (market saturation).

- A technological shift occurs.

- There is a loss of ambition, agility, or innovation as the organization grows larger.

Whatever the cause, few companies sustain high growth rates for more than a decade. This does not mean that growth necessarily stops and that continued financing is not needed. Even saturated markets for mature products, such as automobiles, continue to expand incrementally as the population increases and as people in undeveloped countries become more affluent and demand them. For a $1 billion enterprise, even a 3 percent growth in revenues may require additional financing. Then, too, mature companies are often involved in mergers, acquisitions, restructuring, or other activities, all of which have important financing implications.

Assuming that the mature company is creditworthy, it has many options for obtaining additional external funds. For short-term needs, it can issue commercial paper, tap its bank line of credit, or negotiate a term loan with a bank or other financial institutions, such as insurance companies and pension funds. The mature company can use its existing assets and cash flow as collateral to lower the cost of loans. Alternatively, the company can obtain significant funds through sale-and-leaseback arrangements.

The healthy, mature company also enjoys access to public capital markets for debt (bonds) and equity capital (stock). Here, timing is all-important. The company naturally wants to sell its bonds when interest rates are low and sell its shares when share prices are high.

Financing Growth at eBay

To better appreciate the sequence of financing experienced by growing entrepreneurial enterprises, consider eBay, perhaps the most successful company of the dot-com age. It exploded from a home-based hobby business to a sizable corporation in a very short time. The company's early history (1995 through 2000) illustrates the role played by various forms of financing.

eBay was started in 1995 by Pierre Omidyar, a young man with experience in software development and online commerce. Omidyar set up his business on a free Web site provided by his Internet service. His only business assets at the time were a filing cabinet, an old school desk, and a laptop computer. Omidyar's hobby-business grew quickly, and that forced him to buy his own server, hire someone to handle billings and the checks that came in the mail, and eventually move the operation from his apartment to a small office. Omidyar and his business partner, Jeff Skoll, soon began paying themselves annual salaries of $25,000.[3]

This early period of growth was essentially self-financed: The cash coming in the mail from transaction fees was sufficient to cover the business's expenses and investments. But a period of hypergrowth was right around the corner. By the end of December 2000, this little online company had grown from serving a handful of auction devotees to dealing with the transactions of twenty-two million registered users. By then it offered more than eight thousand product categories; on any given day, the company listed more than six million items for sale in an auction-style format, and another eight million items in a fixed-price format.

An infrastructure of office space, customer support, proprietary software, information systems, and equipment was required to host a business with this volume and keep it churning. eBay developed systems to operate its auction service and to process transactions, including billing and collections. Those systems had to be continually improved and expanded as the pace of transactions on the site increased.

To keep the wheels of growth turning, the company spent liberally on new site features and categories. eBay reported $4.6 million in product development expenses in 1998, $24.8 million in 1999, and $55.9 million in 2000. Even larger sums were spent on marketing, brand development, and acquisitions aimed at broadening the company's services and extending its reach to other parts of the world.

Before long, eBay had expanded its balance-sheet assets dramatically. Here are a few highlights (rounded to millions) from the company's 10-K report for the fiscal year ending December 31, 2000:

Cash and cash equivalents: $202 million

Short-term investments: $354 million

Long-term investments: $218 million

Total assets: $1,182 million

With total assets of nearly $1.2 billion, eBay was light-years away from Pierre Omidyar's apartment operation. Where did the money come from to finance those assets? eBay's remarkable growth was principally financed in two ways: first, by cash flows from operations (self-financing) and, second, by loans and the sale of ownership shares (external financing). Let's examine these sources individually, because they are important to growing companies.

eBay's Cash Flows from Operations

In the early days, cash flow from operations was an important source of growth financing. The company's cash flow statement—which totals the cash flow entering and leaving the enterprise as a result of operations, investments, and financing activities—documents the effect of internally generated financing. (If you are unfamiliar with the cash flow statement, see appendix A.) Table 6-5 contains the highlights of eBay's cash flow statement for 1998 through 2000.

The first row, net cash provided by operating activities, shows that the company ran some portion of its operations and paid people's salaries, taxes, and other bills (operating activities) from operating cash flow. What's more, the level of positive cash flow from operations grew substantially from year to year, helping to fund

TABLE 6-5

eBay's Cash Flow, 1998 through 2000 (in Thousands of Dollars)

	2000	1999	1998
Net Cash Provided by Operating Activities	100,148	62,852	6,041
Net Cash Used in Investing Activities	(206,054)	(603,363)	(53,024)
Net Cash Provided by Financing Activities	85,978	725,027	72,159
Net Increase (Decrease) in Cash and Cash Equivalents	(19,928)	184,516	25,176
Cash and Cash Equivalents at End of Year (After Accounting for Beginning Balance)	201,873	221,801	37,285

Source: eBay 10-K report, 2000.

growth. Thus, an important portion of eBay's asset growth was financed internally, from its successful and profitable operations. Instead of returning even a cent of that cash to shareholders in the form of dividends, it plowed everything back into the business. That is typical of fast-growing firms.

eBay's External Financing

Internally generated cash was sufficient to finance operations in the early days, but not nearly sufficient to fund eBay's meteoric growth. Large as they were, eBay's operating cash flows paled in comparison with the cash outflows caused by investments during the same period. In the best of those years (2000), cash flow from operations covered slightly less than half of the investment outflow. To make up the difference, the company resorted to external financing (depicted in the line labeled "Net cash provided by financing activities" in table 6–5).

eBay's financial statements, which are too voluminous to show here, indicate that almost all of its external financing took the form of stockholders' capital; that is, the company and its subsidiaries raised cash by selling shares (almost all common shares) to investors. The first of these was a $5 million private placement with Benchmark Capital, a Silicon Valley venture capital firm. In return for its cash, Benchmark was given a 22 percent equity interest in eBay.

The next big capital-raising event in eBay's history was its 1998 initial public offering. An IPO is a major milestone in a corporation's life cycle in that the offering marks the company's transition from a private to a public enterprise. As you'll see in a later chapter, this new status opens up much larger opportunities to raise equity capital. The universe of potential capital contributors expands from the small and clubby circle of private investors to a much broader group of individual investors, mutual funds, and pension funds.

An IPO is also an opportunity for the existing investors, including the venture capitalists and shareholding employees, to cash in some or all of their shares—turning paper certificates into real money. eBay's Omidyar, for example, held more than forty-four million shares of his company's common stock before its IPO. In the wake of the IPO and the stock price run-up in the months that followed, Omidyar became a billionaire four times over. The value of Benchmark's shares rose to the point that it could claim a 49,000 percent return on its investment—one for the record books!

eBay's financial managers and investment bankers used the company's high stock price and public appetite for shares to float yet another common stock issue in 1999. This one netted the company

Follow the Money

This short tale about eBay illustrates a familiar pattern among successful entrepreneurial firms. Start-up funds generally come from the pockets of the founder. Growth is financed by internally generated cash flows and perhaps a modest bank loan; then by the private sale of ownership shares; and eventually in some cases by the sale of shares to the public.

more than $700 million, most of which was used in the company's campaign of expansion.

Other Forms of External Financing

Thus far in this chapter we've described supplier trade credit, bank loans, and common stock issues as important forms of external financing. Today's mature corporations also use a few other important forms of financing:

- **Commercial paper.** Large corporations with high credit ratings often use the sale of commercial paper to finance their short-term requirements. They use it as a lower-cost alternative to short-term bank borrowing. *Commercial paper* is a short-term debt security, generally reaching maturity in two to two hundred seventy days. Most paper is sold at a discount from its face value and is redeemable at face value on maturity. The difference between the discounted sale price and the face value represents interest to the purchaser of the paper. Investors having temporary cash surpluses are the usual purchasers of commercial paper; for them it is a reasonably safe way to obtain a return on their idle cash.

- **Bonds.** A *bond* is also a debt security (IOU), usually issued with a fixed interest rate and a stated maturity date. The bond issuer has a contractual obligation to make periodic interest payments and to redeem the bond at its face value on maturity. Bonds may have short-, intermediate-, or long-term maturities (e.g., from one to thirty years). Generally, they pay a fixed interest rate on a semiannual basis.

- **Preferred stock.** This type of equity security is similar to a bond in that it pays a stated dividend to the shareholder each year, and after the shares begin trading in the secondary market, then the share prices, like bonds, fluctuate with changes in market interest rates and the creditworthiness of the issuer. Also like bonds, *preferred stock* is used by some corporations as an external form of equity financing.

Matching Assets and Financing

One of the principles of financing—whether to start a company, maintain its operations, or advance its growth—is to make a proper match between the assets and their associated forms of financing. The general principle is to finance current (short-term) assets with short-term financing, and long-term assets with long-term or permanent financing.

The use of supplier trade credit for financing inventory, as described earlier in this chapter, is an example of matching short-term assets with short-term financing. The shoe-store owner matched sixty-day financing against an asset expected to be sold within that period. Similarly, companies finance their infrastructure of office space, systems, and equipment with either long-term debt or capital supplied by shareholders—more permanent forms of financing.

Countless enterprises follow this sensible principle. When states and municipalities build bridges, hockey stadiums, water treatment plants, and so forth, they typically finance them with twenty- to thirty-year bonds—financing vehicles whose maturities roughly match the productive life of the assets.

To understand why this principle is important, consider first what might happen if you tried to finance the purchase of your new home (a long-term asset) with an 8 percent, nonamortizing $200,000 loan that came due in only three years. Under the terms of the loan, you'd pay $16,000 in annual interest and then would be obligated to repay the $200,000 at the end of the third year. This would be feasible *if* you could negotiate another loan at the end of three years to replace the one that's due and *if* interest rates were still affordable. But that's two *if*'s. Money might become so tight that you could not locate a new lender when you needed one, or the lender you found might want 10 or 12 percent. In either case, foreclosure would be likely. You couldn't operate with such a situation, and neither can a business enterprise.

The opposite mismatch situation—borrowing long to finance a short-term asset—is just as bad. Some people take out second mortgages on their homes to finance a dream vacation. Such are the temptations of home equity loans. The vacation will soon be over, but the payments will go on and on. In business, we expect that the assets we acquire with borrowed money will produce incremental revenues (or cost savings) at rates and over periods more than sufficient to pay their financing costs. The same can be said for owners' capital.

Summing Up

- A lifestyle enterprise is a business whose goal is to provide income and a retirement nest egg for the founder. Its start-up phase, if it survives, is followed perhaps by a period of gradual growth, followed by a no-growth phase of maturity.

- Start-up phase financing, for both lifestyle and entrepreneurial enterprises, is generally bootstrapped from personal savings, credit cards, friends and family, and in some cases by small bank loans.

- Trade credit from suppliers is another low-cost source of financing.

- Bankers look to a borrower's ability to repay, character, and collateral before making a loan.

- The current ratio, the acid-test ratio, and the times interest paid ratio give lenders insights into the ability of a prospective borrower to repay a loan.

- Entrepreneurial firms generally rely on bootstrap financing to get them through the start-up phase.

- Growth phase entrepreneurs look to internally generated cash flow, asset-based loans, and external equity capital for financing.

- Debt is generally the lowest-cost form of capital because interest payments are tax deductible; however, carrying debt makes an enterprise riskier.

- A public issuing of shares (initial public offering) is a major milestone for the few entrepreneurial firms that reach it. An IPO provides a major infusion of cash to fuel growth.

- Maturity phase financing for creditworthy companies may include bank loans and the sale of commercial paper, bonds, and stock.

- It's best to finance short-term assets with short-term financing, and long-term assets with long-term debt or shareholders' contribution.

Angels and Venture Capitalists

For Serious Outside Equity

Key Topics Covered in This Chapter

- *why external capital is often necessary*

- *how to approach business angels for capital*

- *what attracts venture capitalists*

- *the venture capital process*

- *locating and connecting with VCs*

- *tips for making hard-hitting presentations to angels and venture capitalists*

- *the pros and cons of venture capital funding*

MANY BUSINESSES NEVER get to the point of needing or wanting outside equity capital. The founders can use internally generated cash and loans to expand the enterprise to a size that, to them, is manageable and satisfactory. Best of all, this route avoids selling a share of ownership to outsiders. Generally, these are the lifestyle businesses described earlier. According to scholar William E. Wetzel Jr., these firms produce revenues of less than $10 million after five years and account for more than 90 percent of start-up businesses in the United States.[1]

Other entrepreneurs raise their sights higher. In Wetzel's classification, these are middle-market firms that shoot for $10 million to $50 million in revenues after five years, and what he calls high-potential firms that aim for $50 million and up.[2] Both of these types of more aggressive enterprises must at some point seek equity capital from outside investors to finance growth. Debt financing and internally generated cash are rarely feasible solutions.

Equity capital is capital that provides rights of ownership. Equity capital gives its contributor an ownership interest in the assets of the enterprise and a share of its future fortunes. In most cases it gives the contributor a voice in how the business should be run. This chapter describes the two most immediate sources of equity capital that come from people outside the business after friends and relatives have been considered: business angels and venture capitalists. It explains how you can connect with them and discusses the pros and cons of taking their money.

Business Angels

If all your information came from the financial media, you'd assume that venture capital (VC) firms provide most of the equity funding used by entrepreneurial companies during their developmental stages—that is, before they issue their first shares to the public. It is true that a few firms having huge growth potential connect with VCs almost immediately—long before they have marketable products or services. But lifestyle and middle-market ventures never show up on the radar of venture capitalists. And only a small percentage of high-potential businesses obtain venture funding. Instead, many, if not most, middle- and high-potential ventures obtain equity capital from a class of investors called *business angels*. Researchers Mark Van Osnabrugge and Robert J. Robinson, in fact, estimate that angels provide thirty to forty times more financing to entrepreneurial firms each year than do venture capitalists.[3]

Who are these business angels? They are high-net-worth individuals, usually successful businesspeople or professionals, who provide early-stage capital to start-up businesses in the form of either debt, equity capital, or both. They provide financing for start-up and early-stage firms that are

- too small to get the attention of VC firms

- often too limited in their revenue potential at maturity to interest VC firms

- too risky for bank loans and for most VC appetites

Thus, business angels are VCs with a lowercase *v*. And they fill a huge financing void.

Angels are often self-made millionaires and are accustomed to taking calculated risks with their own money—risks that have the potential of producing exceptional returns. Many enjoy the game of finding and exploiting commercial opportunities. Consider this example:

Jack is a sixty-two-year-old Minneapolis businessman. He doesn't have an M.B.A.; in fact, Jack never went to college. What he does have *is a profitable short-haul trucking and truck maintenance company with $43 million in annual revenues. He built that business from the ground up. He also owns minority interests in two other successful businesses in the area and is an active member of their boards.*

Financially secure and confident of his business acumen, Jack enjoys learning about investment opportunities in the Minneapolis area and taking active investment positions in the ones that he likes and understands. In some cases, Jack has joined forces with two close friends— both wealthy businesspeople—in these investments. One is a long-time friend and accountant, the owner of a local CPA firm. The other, a golfing buddy, owns and manages several apartment buildings in the city. "Three minds are better than one," Jack says.

Jack is one of an estimated three hundred fifty thousand business angels in the United States. According to Jeffrey Sohl, a professor at the University of New Hampshire's Center for Venture Research, angels invested between $30 billion and $35 billion in almost fifty thousand ventures in the United States alone in 2001.[4]

Assuming that you have a solid business plan and the know-how to launch and operate a successful company, people like Jack and his friends represent your best opportunity to secure substantial outside capital. And money is not the only thing they have to offer. Business angels are successful people who can contribute advice and feedback when you need it. They also have valuable local networks that can be helpful to you. Whether you need to find a good attorney, accounting services, a banker, a supplier, a key employee, or office space, your angel can usually put you in touch with reliable people.

Connecting with Angels

Ironically, even though business angels are probably living in or near your community, they aren't always easy to spot. Unlike venture capital firms, angels do not advertise themselves. And like most self-made people, they keep their investment activities to themselves and their circle of trusted associates. There is a good chance that you already know or do business with one or several angels without realizing it.

So how can you bring your financing needs to the attention of business angels in your area? Perhaps the best approach is to find a way into their network—through your lawyer, your accountant, or other entrepreneurs of your acquaintance. Talk with patent attorneys. Show your business plan to the right people. Whisper in the right ears. Doing these things may get the word out to the right people in the local angel network.

A more affirmative approach is to ask successful entrepreneurs in your area, "Whom should I approach about private financing?" If the person they suggest cannot help you, ask that person the same question: "Do you know anyone who might want to invest in my company?" Follow every lead until you connect with the right person or persons.

Organized Angels

Business angels traditionally have operated individually or in small, informal, and collegial groups. This is changing as angels create organizations and networks. As reported in *Inc. Magazine,* some one hundred seventy angel groups have been formed in the United States over the past several years. A list of these groups, by state, with their Web sites, can be found at www.angelsummit.org.

These groups are making angel investing more professional, more formal, and—for the angels—more efficient. In some ways they are becoming more like venture capital firms, with professional screeners doing some of the legwork and initial analysis. The benefit of these organizations for entrepreneurs is that they are making the chore of finding and contacting a potential financier less time-consuming and less hit-or-miss.

European angels are also becoming better organized. The European Business Angels Network (EBAN) is a nonprofit association that aims to encourage the exchange of experience among angel investors (www.eban.org). EBAN estimates that there are business angel investment pools of 3 billion euros in the U.K., 20 million in Ireland, 1.5 billion in the Netherlands, and 300 million in Finland. It has no data on other European countries.[5] In Australia, Business Angels Pty Ltd (www.businessangels.com.au) provides a central register that solves some of the difficulties that private investors and companies have in finding each other. Its database matches business needs with the criteria of private investors.

Tips for Getting Angel Financing

- Don't waste your time looking for an angel if you cannot make a case that your business will create annual revenues in excess of $10 million to $15 million within five years. Few angels are interested in businesses that cannot reach that level.

- Look for angels in professions related to your enterprise. For example, if yours is an information systems start-up, hunt for people whose wealth was made in that industry. For example, one of the founders of Sun Microsystems saw a prelaunch demonstration of Google's search engine and gave that company's grad student entrepreneurs a check for $100,000. As a seasoned computing professional, he was able to appreciate its potential. If you hope to build a business around a new medical device, get the word out to local physicians.

- Have your act together: either a working prototype, a well-managed and lean operation, or, at a minimum, a rock-solid business plan.

- Be ready with a well-rehearsed, right-to-the-point verbal presentation. You should be prepared to explain clearly and specifically how the angel's money will be used to fuel profitable growth.

- Have a credible exit plan for your investors. Angels want to eventually convert their paper ownership interests into real money.

Venture Capitalists

Whereas business angels generally stay in the shadows of new business financing, venture capitalists have a far more visible presence. A *venture capitalist* is an individual or firm that seeks large capital gains by providing early-stage equity or equity-linked financing to high-potential entrepreneurial opportunities—opportunities that can eventually be harvested for substantial profits. The enterprises that attract the VC represent less than 1 percent of all business start-ups. In fact, it is highly unlikely that a VC firm will even skim your business plan if you don't have one or more people on the management team who have successfully created a hugely successful enterprise, as well as an upside opportunity of huge sales revenues.

The vast majority of enterprises that attract VCs are technology-driven businesses: software, hardware, and Internet-related. The life sciences and biotech also manage to capture a share of VC money, as do the few retail situations, such as Staples, that have the potential to quickly expand store locations and dominate their markets. What is hot with venture capitalists changes with the times: from microprocessor companies in the 1970s to biotech and cellular telecommunications in the 1980s. During the 1990s, VCs financed hundreds of dot-com companies, most of which no longer exist, proving that even smart people with money are susceptible to a "great story" and lemming-like behavior.

The businesses that most attract VCs tend to be risky ones with proven management and substantial growth potential. For these financiers, a first-rate person with a good idea is far more attractive than a good idea with second-rate management. Many of the companies they focus on haven't yet developed a marketable product or service. And because investments in these companies lack immediate liquidity, the VCs anticipate that their funds will be tied up for several years.

In the venture capitalist's mind, high risk and illiquidity are offset by high potential payoffs. For example, Arthur Rock's $1.5 million investment in fledgling Apple Computer was risky, but it was valued at $100 million three years later when the company went public. A $25 million VC investment in a small overnight delivery service called Federal Express was worth $1.2 billion at the time of the company's initial public offering of shares. Venture capitalists are always looking for the next Staples, Dell, Intuit, Amgen, or Starbucks. It's what they live for. Consequently, if your venture lacks the potential to take them to the moon, your search for VC financing will probably be fruitless.

The Venture Capital Process

If capital from this source is a realistic prospect, it is useful to know where venture capital money comes from, how the capital flow to high-potential firms is managed, and how returns are distributed. Scholar-practitioners William Bygrave and Jeffry Timmons have described this through a funds flow diagram shown here as figure 7-1. The VC firm shown here is a limited partnership in which passive limited partners contribute most of the capital. These partners may be wealthy individuals, pension funds, university endowments, or corporations. For them, risky venture financing constitutes a small part of their overall portfolios.

The venture capital firm acts as the (active) general partner, employing a cadre of bright new M.B.A.'s, securities lawyers, and experienced deal makers to identify, screen, and invest in high-potential firms identified in figure 7-1 as portfolio companies. The wise VC firm will diversify its bets among many deals, knowing that some will fail and others will only break even, but maybe one in fifteen will be the bonanza that makes them rich. As a practical approach to diversification, VC firms form small syndicates in which the lead investor conducts the due diligence and takes a seat on the entrepreneurial company's board. Other members of the syndicate contribute smaller amounts to the total financing and generally take a passive approach to the investment.

The VC's capital contribution often takes the form of convertible preferred stock. This stock has voting rights—something that gives the VC a measure of control over the enterprise and its officers—and the terms of the deal give preferred shareholders the right

FIGURE 7-1

The Flow of Venture Capital

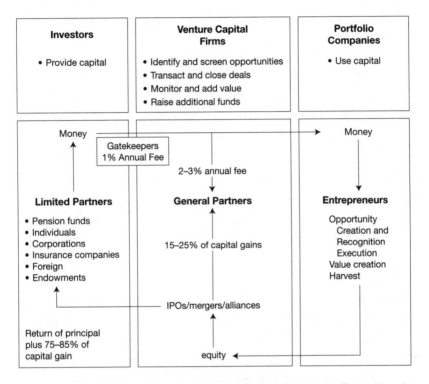

Source: William D. Bygrave and Jeffry A. Timmons, *Venture Capital at the Crossroads* (Boston: Harvard Business School Press, 1992), 11. Reproduced with permission.

to convert their securities to common shares at their discretion. Conversion will be stipulated at 1:1 or some other ratio. As preferred shareholders, they are entitled to cumulative dividends that must be paid before any dividends can be paid to common shareholders.

VCs love this type of arrangement because preferred shareholders stand ahead of common shareholders in the event of liquidation. This reduces some of their risk. Meanwhile, the conversion feature allows them to participate in the upside potential of the company. In effect, convertible preferred shareholder status gives VCs the best of both worlds: some protection in the case of business failure, and the right to enjoy whatever success the company produces. (A common alternative to convertible preferred shares is convertible debt with warrants.)

After an investment is made, the venture capitalist does three things:

1. Monitors the progress of its portfolio companies

2. Uses its network of contacts to help portfolio companies strengthen their technical and management teams

3. Shapes company plans and strategies through its influence on their boards

The end of the venture capital process comes when the VC harvests part or all of its investment, usually when its portfolio companies go public or are purchased by other corporations. During the dot-com bubble—and before the bubble burst—this opportunity often came within a year or two. In normal times, harvest typically comes after four or five years. The investors and the VC firms share in harvested profits according to the terms of their partnership.[6]

Connecting with Venture Capitalists

If your enterprise meets its criteria, there's a chance that a venture capitalist firm might find you before you find it. Competitive VCs go hunting for promising deals. They keep in touch with people located in high-tech spawning beds such as MIT's research labs and Stanford University, and they work entrepreneurial networks in Silicon Valley, in North Carolina's research triangle, among San Diego's biotech community, and so forth. But if you need venture capital, you cannot wait for them to find you. And you cannot wait until you really need a cash infusion; you should line up venture money six or eight months before it is actually needed.

One approach to connecting with a VC is to get a directory of venture capital firms and send the executive summary of your business plan via e-mail to each one that specializes in your area: life science, computers, or whatever it happens to be. Don't bother sending the entire plan; they don't have time to read it. If the VC is intrigued by your executive summary, he or she will ask for the entire plan. This underscores the importance of writing a clear and compelling executive summary!

Unfortunately, sending out blind e-mails is about as effective as sending out blind résumés when you're hunting for a job. Neither is likely to produce the desired result. To the VC, you are only one of thousands of faceless supplicants. The way to change this perception and improve your odds is to make it personal—that is, find a way to personally meet the VC or have your case recommended by someone the VC respects. Here are a few techniques:

- Attend entrepreneurial forums. Cities with many high-tech start-ups periodically hold events that bring entrepreneurs and financiers together. Typically, each of many VC firms has a separate table, and each eager entrepreneur is given a five- to ten-minute opportunity to visit each and make the pitch. Attend these forums whenever possible. But be totally prepared. Have a brief but compelling elevator speech about the opportunity you've identified and how your team intends to exploit it.

- Be ready with a twenty-minute presentation. Whenever you make contact with a venture capitalist (as just discussed), ask for an opportunity to come to the office and make a presentation. That presentation should be brief, well organized, compelling, and well rehearsed. Deliver the highlights, and be prepared to supply the details if asked.

- Have the right people on your team. The venture capitalist may not know you or your company, but if he or she knows and respects someone on your team or your board of directors, you may get a face-to-face meeting. Keep this in mind as you form your management team and select advisers and board members. Use an attorney who is highly respected by local VCs. All other things being equal, select board members who have personal connections to financiers.

VC Locators

Pratt's Guide to Venture Capital Sources, edited by Stanley E. Pratt and available at Amazon.com, is a comprehensive listing of venture capital sources. It is organized in a way that you can quickly locate VCs having the desired characteristics and interests. This $475 book is updated periodically. An online version is also available.

Also on the Web (at http://web.vcgate.com), VCgate offers an extensive directory of venture capital, private equity, merchant banking, and other investment firms from around the world. The VCgate database, which purports to include some three thousand eight hundred listings from the United States, Canada, Europe, and Asia, makes searching quick and efficient.

Making a Presentation

Assuming that you are successful in making contact with an angel or venture capitalist and have been invited to make a presentation about your company, how should you handle it? An opportunity like this doesn't come along every day, so you cannot afford to botch it. First Capital Advisors, L.C., a Provo, Utah, firm that helps entrepreneurs secure capital, offers the ten tips shown in figure 7-2 for making hard-hitting presentations.

Rehearse your presentation until you have it down cold. You must convey the impression that you are in control of the facts and that you have great confidence in the company and its future. After you have made the presentation, says First Capital Advisors, expect some pointed questions from your audience. Anticipate their key questions and have rock-solid answers for each one.

A Caveat on Taking VC Capital

Angels and VCs can provide the capital that every successful business eventually needs to grow to its full potential. They are also sources of

FIGURE 7-2

Ten Tips for Effective Presentations

1. Don't hand out anything until the presentation is over—your audience will paw through the materials and not listen to you.

2. Explain the deal right at the start. For example: "We are raising $500,000 by selling common shares at $1 per share—that represents a 20 percent stake in the company." Prospective financiers will want to know how you came up with the 20 percent figure and why you priced it at $1 per share.

3. How is the company valued and how did you figure it out? (In the above example the company would have a $2.5 million valuation.)

4. Who currently owns what shares or percentage, and what did they put into the company in return for those shares? What options or warrants have been issued or proposed?

5. Explain the idea and competitive niche as if your prospective investors were customers to whom you were selling the product or service. Don't give a technical explanation.

6. A chronological marketing plan is critical. Explain in detail, not in generalities, how you are going to produce sales.

7. Describe the use of the proceeds. How will the investors' monies be used?

8. Explain why the current management team will be successful and, if they have a long string of successes, why you don't have big dollars of your own. Why do you need the angel's or the VC's money?

9. Don't tell them that the exit strategy is going to be an IPO or a private sale to another company or merger unless someone on your management team has done this before, or unless you have details as to how the goal would be accomplished. If you say that you are going to do an IPO, have an idea as to who would be your underwriters, SEC-qualified auditors, and securities attorneys. And have a comprehensive timetable.

10. Have your current financials available for examination, no matter how ugly they are.

Source: First Capital Advisors, L. C. Adapted with permission.

useful advice and, through their personal networks, can provide access to suppliers, strategic partners, and managerial talent. For any company that looks forward to an initial public offering, having a venture capitalist on its side is almost essential. A good VC firm has the sophistication, connections, and experience to get an initial public offering off the ground and on terms that maximize shareholder value.

The benefits of outside capital, however, carry a heavy cost. Venture capital can be the most expensive form of capital you can use. Consider eBay, which took $5 million from Benchmark Capital in return for 22 percent of company ownership. Whereas a commercial

How Much of Your Company Should the VC Get?

If a venture capitalist firm likes your company and its prospects, it might agree to making a cash infusion via convertible preferred stock or some type of convertible debt, as described earlier. But because the VC can convert to common shares at its option, it is really taking a share of ownership. The question is, What share of total ownership should the VC receive in return for its money? Should $5 million entitle the VC to 20 percent of share ownership? Or 40 percent? Or 51 percent?

This is one of the most critical issues for the entrepreneur and hinges on the estimated value of the firm. If the VC says, "We've estimated the value of your company at $6 million," ask for a detailed explanation of how that figure was determined. Valuation is part science and part art. And because the VC firm is much more experienced in both, it has a negotiating advantage over the entrepreneur. To level the playing field, wise entrepreneurs will bring in professional assistance to develop their own assessments of enterprise value. This is the best assurance that an equitable division of ownership is made.

The methodologies used in business valuation can be very complex—too complex to cover in this chapter. Nevertheless, you owe it to yourself to be acquainted with them. (For an overview of the methods typically used, see Appendix C of this book.)

bank might have made $2 million in interest from a loan of that size over three years, eBay's VCs chalked up a 49,000 percent return, more than $2 billion, in the same period. True, Benchmark did help the young company recruit an effective and experienced CEO and other members of the management team, but a good executive recruiter would have done the same for less than $200,000. The VC also played a major role in arranging for the company's successful IPO, but was that work worth $2 billion when investment banking advice can be obtained on a consulting basis for a reasonable fee? The lesson: Venture capital is free if the enterprise fails, but it can be enormously costly to the entrepreneur if the business succeeds.

There is also the matter of control and possible conflicts of interest. VCs with a major stake in a business can make the founder's life miserable if the two cannot work together harmoniously. It may even have enough control to "fire" the founder. Also, the VC's vision might be to quickly flip the company through an IPO or to sell the business to a big corporation, cash in its investment, and move on. The founder, on the other hand, may wish to remain private for a while longer and build the enterprise in line with a long-term vision.

For these reasons many entrepreneurs look upon venture capitalists as a necessary evil or, in the worst cases, as "venture vultures." Table 7-1 summarizes the pros and cons of venture capital that every entrepreneur should consider.

TABLE 7-1

Pros and Cons of Using Venture Capital

Pros	Cons
• A successful model for financing business growth and development.	• VCs may demand a majority position (51 percent).
• A necessary evil. Angels, grants, and corporate money may be too little, too late.	• VC 51 percent ownership disqualifies a company from SBIR grants.
• VC will help to maximize long-term shareholder value	• VC will likely base offer on a low valuation and offer financial terms unfavorable to the owner: "vulture" capital.
• Assists rapid progress in product development, etc.	• Few deals recently. VCs are being extremely selective and slow.
• The VC's deep pockets can rescue the company if there is a setback.	• VCs strongly prefer later-stage companies to start-ups.
• VC will facilitate an initial public offering.	• VC's board position may be less useful than promised (some sit on a dozen boards and spend the rest of their time evaluating new deals).
• VCs add validation and prestige in the eyes of corporate partners and follow-on investors.	
• VC sits on the board, adding value and focus.	
• VCs are smart, experienced entrepreneurs with track records (e.g., former CEOs).	

Source: Michael C. Luecke, adapted with permission.

A fast-growing business with huge growth potential can hardly avoid using outside equity capital, but others can—or can delay its necessity while they build real value for themselves. Here are a few tips for doing so:

- Rely as heavily as possible on bootstrap financing. This type of financing doesn't force you to give up ownership.

- Manage growth at a pace you can handle with existing financing—that is, through a combination of internally generated cash flow, bootstrapping, loans, and partnerships with customers and suppliers.

- Be tightfisted with the money you have. Keep expenses low, and find every opportunity for doing more with less.

- Outsource nonessential functions whenever possible. This will allow you to do more with less capital. The modern economy is flush with contract manufacturers and assemblers, fulfillment houses, information systems, and even firms that will handle all transactional aspects of your human resource function.

Entrepreneurs should also realize that the more solid their business is when they negotiate with outside investors, the better deal they will make for themselves. Instead of giving away the company—and control—they'll keep more of it for themselves. A viable business that isn't desperate for money can obtain much better terms.

Learn More

Negotiating with venture capitalists is a high-stakes game for the founder-entrepreneur. To learn more about the issues involved and to find out how you can be a more effective negotiator, see the reference to the case note "Venture Capital Negotiations: VC Versus Entrepreneur" in the "For Further Reading" section of this book.

Summing Up

- The most likely source of outside venture funding comes from so-called business angels.

- Angels are high-net-worth individuals who provide early-stage capital to start-up businesses.

- Networking is often the best way to connect with business angels.

- A venture capitalist is an individual or firm that seeks large capital gains through early-stage equity or equity-linked financing of high-potential entrepreneurial enterprises.

- Entrepreneurs should not waste their time pursuing VC money unless they have all the characteristics VCs look for.

- Most VC capital takes the form of convertible preferred stock or something similar, such as convertible debt with warrants.

- VC money is nice to have, but it is costly in both economic terms and loss of control of the enterprise.

8

Going Public

Adventures in the Capital Markets

Key Topics Covered in This Chapter

- *the pros and cons of going public*

- *what it takes to be an IPO candidate*

- *the role of investment bankers*

- *eight steps to doing a deal*

- *the private placement alternative*

A T SOME POINT, growing firms with exceptional revenue potential seek financing through an initial public offering (IPO) of their ownership shares to the world of individual investors and institutional investors such as pension funds and mutual funds. That event results in a significant exchange of paper ownership shares for the hard cash the firm needs for stability and expansion.

An IPO marks a major milestone in the life of a company. It signals that the enterprise has earned the confidence of people outside its inner circle of participants, and it makes the enterprise accountable to a much broader universe of stakeholders, analysts, and regulators.

Perhaps fewer than 5 percent of readers will have any direct use for the information contained in this chapter because only a tiny fraction of start-up companies ever go public. Few entrepreneurial companies ever reach the point where an IPO is either necessary or feasible; nevertheless, the rewards of this form of financing make it intensely interesting to company founders, key employees, and early-stage contributors of capital. So read on if you're curious, or skip to the next chapter if you're short on time.

This chapter examines the pros and cons of becoming a public company and explores what it takes to be a candidate for this form of financing. Investment bankers play a critical role in preparing the IPO and getting the deal done. An overview of that role is provided here. The chapter also gives an overview of the IPO process itself, from planning through the actual deal. Finally, the chapter examines the post-deal environment.

A Note on Legalities

This chapter is written from the perspective of U.S. companies and U.S. securities laws and procedures. Readers outside the United States should consult their own securities laws and procedures.

Pros and Cons of Going Public

You've probably read many accounts of founders and key employees of entrepreneurial companies who had quite ordinary financial circumstances the day before their firms went public. By the end of the next day those same individuals were millionaires. What a difference a day makes!

Founder Pierre Omidyar, for example, owned the equivalent of forty-four million common shares on the eve of eBay's IPO in 1998—pieces of paper for which there was no market. He was living in a rented house and driving an old Jetta. The next day those shares began trading on NASDAQ and began a long upward ascent. Before long, Omidyar's paper shares had a market value in excess of $4 billion. Other employees and early-stage investors shared in the wealth.

But something else happened the day eBay's shares began trading. Some changes were positive, but others were negative.

Pros

Gaining personal wealth is one of the benefits of going public, but it is not the only one. The liquidity provided by marketability gives the founder and shareholding employees the liquidity they need to raise their standards of living, plan their estates more effectively, and diversify their assets. At the same time, the cash that flows onto the company's balance sheet from the IPO has these positive effects:

- Costly interest-bearing debt can be paid off.

- The company has the financial capacity to develop new products and the marketing capabilities to sell them.

- An improved debt/equity ratio makes it possible, if needed, to obtain debt financing on better terms than otherwise would have been possible.

- Cash and the company's own marketable shares can be used to finance strategic acquisitions.

- The financial stability of the enterprise is improved, making it possible to attract talent, suppliers, and joint-venture partners.

- Becoming a public company opens the door to future rounds of financing through stock and bond sales.

Note: An IPO does not give absolute liquidity to company insiders. U.S. securities regulations place certain restrictions on the sale of insider-owned shares.

Cons

The proceeds from an IPO provide important benefits for owners and investors, but as many a CEO and CFO will attest, public company status is a mixed blessing. Yes, they get the money, but they get a few other things they would rather not have. They must now write a "Dear Shareholders . . ." letter every reporting period. But that's the least of it. Here are the most important drawbacks of becoming a public corporation:

- **The IPO expense.** Just getting the IPO through SEC registration and off the ground generates major legal, accounting, printing, and advisory expenses. Then there are SEC and state securities filing fees and payments to the exchange that lists the stock.

- **Management time and attention.** The preparation that goes into an IPO absorbs an enormous amount of top management time and attention over several months. So too does the *road show*, which takes the CEO and CFO on a time-consuming and costly jaunt to investor meetings around the country. Even after the deal, these two officers must devote part of their time to handling inquiries from investors and security analysts. The company may have to create a position for an investor relations manager to deal with these new stakeholders.

- **Public scrutiny.** The company is now an open book. Its financial results and the compensation of key executives are available to anyone who is interested. The company's 10-K filing will contain information that competitors are bound to find valuable: the names of key suppliers, product development plans, overall strategy, and so forth.

- **Dilution.** Selling shares to the public usually results in a major dilution of ownership by the founder and key managers. Blocks of company stocks are now owned by outsiders, mostly institutional investors. And there may now be thousands of small owners with fewer than one thousand shares.

- **Pressure for short-term gain.** Although most CEOs deny it, the expectations of analysts and investors for predictable year-to-year earnings gains can put decision makers in a difficult position. They may be reluctant to take steps to ensure long-term benefits if doing so will jeopardize short-term results.

The Makings of an IPO Candidate

Do the benefits of being a public company outweigh the drawbacks? Sometimes they do, and sometimes they don't. Even if they do, your enterprise may not be a candidate for an IPO. In fact, an IPO is a pipe dream for all but a small percentage of corporations. This section recounts some of the factors you need to consider before counting your enterprise as an IPO candidate.

Through most of the post–World War II era, U.S. companies didn't go public until they had established a solid record of sales and earnings. After all, investors in an IPO are asked to buy shares of a money-making machine; they want evidence that the machine actually works.

The conservative practice of requiring a record of sales and earnings is occasionally set aside when a company owns proprietary technology and has a tested management team. Investors are willing in these cases to gamble that the company's potential will produce profitable results. During rare periods—the mid- to late 1990s being one—companies with nothing more than a clever idea were able to sell initial public shares. Many of these companies failed to demonstrate their worth in the years that followed.

Thus, the ability to launch a public offering is to a certain extent a function of investor moods and expectations. However, during normal times, when investors are neither hiding in bunkers nor under the influence of mind-altering substances, entrepreneurial firms need these characteristics to be viable IPO candidates:

- A credible CEO who can communicate the enterprise's vision to cautious outsiders.

- A reasonable deal size. Given the cost of launching an IPO, there's little point in seeking less than $10 million. And if you're raising that much, you must have a solid plan for using it.

- Evidence of growth. The firm should have growing sales, with evidence that earnings will follow. Investors expect rising stock prices as a result of double-digit growth in sales and earnings growth at a higher rate. If the earnings record isn't yet there, all signs should point to substantial profitability in the years ahead. This growth should support a price/earning multiple higher than the historical S&P 500 or the Russell 2000.

- Outstanding products or services that are difficult to copy.

- High-quality employees.

- A logical strategy for growth.

In a study of successful IPOs, Ernst & Young found one other trait that few would think to consider as a condition of making the transition from private to public company. It found that successful firms begin acting like public companies long before they did the deal: "[These firms] made improvements in their employee incen-

---

Where to Look for IPO Information

Are you curious about the types of companies that are going public this week? Would you like to know how well the share prices of recent deals have held up in the months after they were issued? You can find this and other information at www.hoovers.com/global/ipoc/index.xhtml. This site tells you which companies are poised to go public (are "on deck") at the moment. It provides a thumbnail sketch of these companies, their revenues, the number of employees, the amount of money they are seeking, and so forth. It also allows you to look through a list of companies that have recently gone public; handy price charts reveal at a glance whether shareholders have won or lost money since their issue dates. Check it out.

---

tive programs . . . in strategic planning, internal controls, financial accounting and reporting, executive compensation, and investor relations policies."[1] Investors in these firms were buying ownership in a firm that had the hallmarks of professional management.

The Role of the Investment Bank

Going public is a specialized activity, one that requires unique skills and capabilities that no entrepreneurial firm has (or should have) on its payroll. These skills and capabilities are obtained through an investment bank.

An investment bank is not like the more familiar commercial bank. It is not in the business of taking deposits and making loans. Instead, it acts as an agent and deal maker for business entities seeking capital. In return for a tidy fee of 6 to 10 percent of the offering price, the investment banker does the following:

1. **Helps the issuing corporation get its regulatory act together.** Specifically, it helps the corporation over the stringent regulatory hurdles that go hand in hand with issuing securities. These

include development of a *prospectus.* In its preliminary form, the prospectus provides full disclosure to potential investors about the company, its business, its finances, and the way it intends to use the proceeds of its securities issuance. The preliminary prospectus is called a "red herring."

2. **Sets the price of the securities being offered.** When shares are being offered to the public for the first time, no one knows for certain how they should be priced. Those shares haven't been traded back and forth by willing buyers and sellers, so there is no certainty as to the market-clearing price. The capital-seeking corporation naturally wants its shares priced as high as the market will bear; doing so maximizes the cash going into its coffers. But investors expect a new issue to be priced at a bargain relative to seasoned securities. The investment banker has expertise in this difficult pricing area and must mediate between these disparate objectives.

3. **Arranges for the distribution of shares.** The issuing corporation may have the shares, but the investment banker has access to potential purchasers. By putting together a syndicate of distributing broker-dealers, the investment banker ensures that it can "move the merchandise" into the portfolios of pension funds, mutual funds, and individual investors. In most cases, the investment bank takes the shares off the hands of the issuing corporation at a given price, marks them up to some predetermined profitable level, and uses its own distribution channels and those of its syndicate partners to sell them to the investing public. In this sense the investment banker "underwrites" the risk of selling hundreds of thousands of shares.

The IPO Process in a Nutshell

Now that you understand the pros and cons of going public and whether your firm is a candidate, let's take a look at the process itself. That process has a number of steps; some must be conducted sequentially, whereas others can be handled in parallel. Very briefly, these steps are as follows:

1. Select an underwriter. The underwriter—the investment banker described earlier—will handle the details in collaboration with the management team. In larger deals, there will be one lead underwriter and one or several comanagers.

2. Prepare the registration statement for filing with the Securities and Exchange Commission (SEC). The registration statement is a document required by federal law that forces the applicant company to disclose past business results, information about the company, and the intended use of the proceeds of the IPO.

3. Conduct *due diligence*. Due diligence is the investigation of facts and statements of risk contained in the registration statement; it aims to ensure that those facts and statements are accurate and that other relevant facts have not been omitted. Is the company using an unorthodox accounting convention? Is it involved in any current lawsuits? Has it been granted patents or are patents pending? Due diligence is the responsibility of those who prepare and sign the registration statement.

4. Print and distribute the prospectus (or red herring). The preliminary prospectus is part of the registration statement. It contains information about the company and the intended use of the issue proceeds, and it is sent to prospective investors to generate interest in the deal.

5. Prepare and conduct a road show: a series of meetings, usually held in major cities around the country, at which potential investors can grill the CEO or CFO (or both) about the company and the intended offering of securities.

6. Agree on a final price and the number of shares to be sold. This is one of the most important steps in the process. What is a fractional share of ownership in a particular company actually worth? Important as this question may be, the answer is based as much on art as on science. A price range will be indicated in

the prospectus sent to investors—for example, $15–$20. As the big moment approaches, however, the underwriter will look at demand for the shares, the price that comparable companies managed to get in recent IPOs (if comparables can be found), and the projected earnings of the company itself. It will also suggest a price that will give investors in the newly issued shares a better than even chance of making money on their transactions—that is, a price slightly lower than the price at which the shares are likely to trade in the days immediately after the offering. If the issuing company does not like the price, it can put the brakes on the offering.

7. Commence trading. After the price has been established and the final regulatory loose ends have been tied up, shares can begin trading on the exchange chosen.

8. Close the purchase and sale of the shares. In this final act of the IPO process, stock certificates are delivered to the shareholders, and the underwriter delivers the proceeds (less its fees and expenses) to the issuing company. The company now has its money.

This process generally takes four to five months. If all has gone well, the entrepreneurial firm ends up with a substantial amount of cash in its war chest and is prepared to begin the second stage of its life—that of a publicly traded corporation. The underwriter will try to support that second stage by providing ongoing research to investors on the newly public company. That research keeps the company in the public eye and, if the news continues to be good, supports the share price.

Certainly there is much, much more to the IPO process than described here. For example, there are restrictions on company-generated publicity before, during, and immediately after the filing period, and there are restrictions on the sale of shares by insiders, called "lockup agreements." The rules regarding the issuing of securities in the United States are, indeed, many and arcane—and that is why professional help is essential.

eBay Goes Public: A Brief Case Example

To better understand how the IPO process works, consider the case of eBay, the online auction company (described earlier in this book) that began operations in 1995.

eBay was incorporated in California in May 1996. A year later it sold a 22 percent ownership stake to the venture capital firm Benchmark Capital in return for $5 million. To this point the company's financing had been entirely private—and outside the realm of the main capital markets. Even a subsequent sale of a series of preferred shares was privately placed with a set of well-heeled investors. eBay first tapped the public capital markets in September 1998 with an initial public offering of common stock. How this IPO was accomplished is both typical and instructive.

Like other corporations eager to tap deep pools of equity capital, eBay enlisted the aid of an investment banking firm—in this case, Goldman Sachs. Goldman Sachs was the lead underwriter of a group of investment bankers that included Bancamerica Robertson Stephens and BT Alex. Brown—both major players.

In the period leading up to eBay's IPO, its CEO and CFO conducted a ten-day, twenty-one-city road show, making a series of presentations to the investment community. A road show is standard procedure with equity issues; it is designed to explain the issuing company's business and generate interest in the offering.

The investment climate at that time was decidedly mixed. The Dow Jones Industrial Average was trending downward, and the NASDAQ Composite Index was meandering beneath the 2000 mark. The great high-tech dot-com boom that would lift the NASDAQ composite into the stratosphere was still over the horizon. Nevertheless, believing that the time was right, eBay and its investment bankers went forward with the offering on September 24, 1998. According to the company's 10-K, slightly more than four million shares were sold, and these netted the fledgling company more than $66 million. Those funds went into the war chest that eBay management would use to finance its growth in the years ahead.

eBay's IPO was priced at what now appears a bargain basement level—roughly $8 (as adjusted for subsequent splits). After those shares began trading over the counter, enthusiastic bidding pushed up that price dramatically. The dot-com frenzy that followed, and the fact that eBay was the only major online venture actually making a profit, did the rest. Within six months, the company's share price had multiplied roughly fifteen-fold.

Fast-growing eBay used its high share price as a form of currency to fund a spate of acquisitions. In May 1999, for example, it made three significant acquisitions, each aimed at increasing the breadth of its core business. They included Butterfield & Butterfield, an established live auction house, which eBay acquired for approximately 1.3 million shares of eBay common stock. Kruse International, a specialist in classic car auctions, was another. It too was acquired entirely with eBay common stock. So too was Billpoint, a small company that had developed a billing and payment solution that permitted individuals and small merchants to accept credit cards as payment for Internet-based sales transactions. Not a penny of cash was used in these deals—one of the benefits of being a public company with a high share price.

But eBay's dealings with external investors was far from finished. Like other growing companies, it found it necessary to return to the market for more equity capital, this time in an offering of five million new shares. That 1999 event added more than $713 million in additional equity capital to the balance sheet.

Alternatives to an IPO

As the eBay case demonstrates, an IPO can be just the thing a growing company needs to expand to its potential. But very few companies have the size or growth potential for this type of financing. Some are in industries that are so out of favor with the investing public that the deal would have few takers. Still other companies deliberately forgo IPOs to avoid the negative features associated with being public. Are these companies cut off from substantial equity capital? No. Are their current owners unable to harvest their investments? Again, the answer is no. There are alternatives to an IPO: sale of a large block of equity via a private placement, and sale of the company itself. Let's consider the first of these here and examine company sales in a later chapter.

Private placement refers to the sale of company stock to one or a few private investors instead of to the general public. In many cases, these private investors are sophisticated financial institutions such as insurance companies, pension funds, and endowment funds that seek a higher return than could be obtained from public investing. A key benefit of private placement is that these deals are exempt from SEC registration requirements (although some states have requirements). Thus, the entrepreneurial firm can obtain a sizable piece of capital without the time and expense of a public offering. Nor will its management and business results be subject to the public scrutiny that follows an IPO.

Private placement financing can take a number of forms: senior or subordinated debt, asset-backed debt, and equity. Because these are private deals, the company and the investor may be able to work out arrangements that suit both parties. For example, if debt is the company's preference but the investor insists on an opportunity to share in the firm's upside potential, an investment banker may be able to design a debt instrument with a below-market interest rate (good for the company) but with warrants attached (good for the investor).

The Need for an Investment Banker

Whatever route you take to secure outside capital, be it an IPO or an alternative, be sure to get the advice of an experienced investment banker. Commercial banks and securities broker-dealers have special departments that do this work. Their services are expensive, but they have the technical expertise and the investor contacts you need to make a favorable deal. For more information on this subject, see the sources listed in "For Further Reading" at the end of this book.

A *warrant* is a security that gives the holder the right to purchase common shares of the warrant-issuing company at a stated price for a stated period of time. The stated price is generally set higher than the current valuation of the shares.

Summing Up

- An IPO is a pipe dream for all but a small number of corporations.

- An IPO brings much-needed cash to a growing company and, for its owners, an opportunity to liquidate and diversify their wealth.

- The downside of an IPO is its expense, absorption of management time, dilution of ownership, ongoing public scrutiny, and pressure to produce short-term gains.

- Don't consider an IPO unless your corporation has these qualities: a CEO who knows how to communicate; a deal size of $10 million or more; a record of double-digit growth in revenues and earnings (or earnings clearly ready to follow); outstanding and difficult-to-copy products or services, quality employees, and a logical strategy for growth.

- An investment bank provides two important necessities: the technical knowledge for getting the deal through the registration process, and the sales network needed to distribute the company's shares to the investing public.

- From the perspective of a cash-hungry U.S. corporation, there are eight steps to an IPO: selecting an underwriter, preparing and filing a registration statement with the SEC, conducting due diligence, distributing a preliminary prospectus (or red herring), mounting a road show by top management, determining the share price and number of shares in the issue, beginning trading; and closing the purchase and sale of shares.

- In many cases a private placement is a good alternative to an IPO.

9

Enterprise Growth

The Challenge to Management

Key Topics Covered in This Chapter

- *three key issues in sustaining growth for the entrepreneurial company*

- *different modes of management triggered by growth*

- *options for changing the guard as the company becomes larger and more complex*

GROWTH IS THE goal of every entrepreneurial business, its founders, and its investors. Whereas owners of lifestyle businesses may be content with an operation they can handily manage themselves or with family members, entrepreneurial start-ups look for much more. They yearn for growing revenues, greater market share, and major profitability. A few pursue an even grander vision: to change how people live and work.

Growth, however, is a mixed blessing. As you've seen earlier, infusions of external capital are usually required if the business is to keep pace with growing demand for its product or service. And every dollar of outside capital has a negative effect. Debt capital raises fixed expenses, making the enterprise more risky. Outside equity capital dilutes the founders' ownership—and control.

Finding more capital is only one of the challenges created by growth, and in the end it may not be the most critical. Capital, after all, naturally flows to successful ventures. The larger challenges are found in marketing, strategy, human resources, and—perhaps most of all—in the transition from entrepreneurial to professional management. This chapter addresses these challenges, with emphasis on the entrepreneur and how his or her role must change as the business expands.

The Impact of Growth

Hewlett-Packard Corporation (HP) traces its origin to a small garage in Palo Alto, California. There in 1938, Bill Hewlett and

David Packard developed an audio oscillator. Walt Disney Studios ordered eight units to use in producing sound effects for one of its films, *Fantasia,* and the two young engineers formalized their partnership the next year. The enterprise listed two employees that year—Bill and Dave—and reported $5,369 in revenues.

Within a year HP had more than doubled revenues, hired another employee, and moved into a larger rented workshop. The war years brought military orders for signal-generating equipment—so many orders that the company had to build a new facility and hire more people to handle all the work. By 1943, the height of the war years, HP had 111 people on its payroll and nearly $1 million in revenues.

Founders Hewlett and Packard learned a thing or two about running a business during those early years, and about managing their own transitions from technical whiz kids to leaders and managers. Packard's wartime experience as an Army officer no doubt helped. The two men learned Rule 1: that management is about getting results through people. Their own skills were insufficient; they had to marshal the talents and energy of many employees.

Innovations in electronics and a surging postwar economy created new challenges for these company founders. They had to identify new market opportunities in the peacetime economy and develop strategies for satisfying them. Equally important, Hewlett and Packard had to develop a style of management and a company culture that would attract talented people and encourage them to contribute to the fullest. That style and culture, later dubbed the HP Way, evolved gradually during the late 1940s and early 1950s.

By contemporary standards, the growth of HP from a two-man partnership to a globe-spanning enterprise with almost ninety thousand employees serving nearly a billion customers seems rather slow. Nineteen years crept by before the company reached the milestone of one thousand employees. How the company should grow and how big it should become were matters of intense internal debate in those days, according the company's own chroniclers. Even more remarkable, HP did not become a public company until 1957, nearly two decades after Bill and Dave went to work in their Palo Alto garage. That deliberate pace stands in sharp contrast to the record of recent wunderkind start-ups. Dell, Inc., broke the one-thousand-employee mark in only a few years and sprinted to an IPO in four. The Starbucks experience was similar. And Staples, the office supply superstore chain, launched its IPO only three years after the 1986 opening of its first store in Brighton, Massachusetts.

Your entrepreneurial firm may never become a Hewlett-Packard, and the odds are high that it will never enjoy the skyrocketing growth of Dell, Starbucks, or Staples. Nevertheless, simply breaking out of the start-up phase and experiencing a healthy dose of growth will expose you to the same perilous transitions and challenges experienced by those companies and their founders. Expanded sales trigger growth in all the activities that support sales: materials purchasing, inventory management, manufacturing, logistics, transaction accounting, and after-sales service. Growing sales oblige management to study new channels of distribution, the feasibility of extending product lines, and possible entry into new markets. New customers create a demand for customer service and for strategies to retain their patronage.

Growing sales must also be supported by personnel—on the production line, in shipping, in sales, and in sales support. And with many more employee heads to count, the company must have human resource personnel to handle recruiting, compliance with labor laws, and benefits administration. And don't forget about finance. Without a knowledgeable CFO and accounting staff to keep payments, collections, and spending on an even keel, the enterprise could easily capsize and sink.

Given these many challenges, entrepreneurs should be careful about what they wish for. More than a few promising ventures have failed because they did not manage their way through their initial success. How prepared are you and your management team for success?

Sustaining Growth

Assuming that you've broken out of the start-up phase and are experiencing revenue growth, you must ask yourself three questions:

1. Is our strategy sustainable?

2. Do we have unique advantages that make it possible to expand successfully into other markets?

3. Is scaling up the business a practical possibility?

Ideally, you will have given these questions much thought in planning your business. Even so, you need to revisit them and recalibrate where necessary. Let's consider each in some detail.

Sustainable Strategy

Strategy is, by definition, that which differentiates a business in a way that confers a competitive advantage. Robust revenue growth is evidence that your strategy is working. The question is, How much longer will it continue working? Perhaps your strategy is based on a new and superior product or technology, or on your ability to deliver an ordinary product at a lower price or in a manner that is extremely convenient for customers.

Southwest Airlines' strategy, for example, was to provide frequent, no-frills, short-haul flights at low prices. That was different from what other airlines were offering at the time, and that difference gave SWA a competitive advantage. And because only one other U.S. domestic airline has demonstrated an ability to do the same thing well (JetBlue), SWA's strategy has been remarkably sustainable.

But few strategies are sustainable over the long term. Eventually, some change will undermine the competitive advantage: new regulation, deregulation, the introduction of a new and superior technology, or a new process for making a product faster, cheaper, or better. In other cases, an entrepreneurial firm (such as yours) creates a new market; if that new market is profitable and expanding, others will recognize its potential and enter with products or services of their own.

The market for home video provides an example. When movies on Beta and VHS cassette became available, entrepreneurs opened rental facilities to serve local markets, and many enjoyed growth and profits. But because there were few barriers to entry, competitors quickly entered the field. First, grocery supermarkets and drugstores set up their own video sections. Then national chains with economies of scale and scope got into the game. Before long, the market that local entrepreneurs had enjoyed was filled with competitors offering the same product. Once demand was satisfied, intense competition led to price cuts and lower profitability.

Could this happen to your business?

To sustain growth, keep looking several steps ahead. Determine where the market wave is heading, and then get on the leading edge of the wave. Find ways to bar the door to potential competitors. eBay did this by making massive expenditures on branding and on efforts to quickly establish its online auction site as *the* place to buy and sell merchandise. Its success on those related fronts effectively shut out serious rivals. People who wanted to sell had every reason to list their items on eBay: That's where the most buyers were. Buyers, too, went straight to eBay: That's where they'd find the most items for sale. It became a virtuous circle that competitors couldn't break into.

It's unlikely that eBay's strategy would be appropriate for your business, but there are other ways to be the vendor of choice or to discourage rivals from entering your market. Here are a few:

- Exploit the learning curve. If you are the first in the market, continual improvement in product design and manufacturing efficiency will allow you to offer your item for less and yet maintain the same profitability. Late-to-market competitors that fail to catch you on the learning curve will be doomed to slim profits or none at all.

- Don't price for maximum profits. Competitors are drawn to markets with high profit margins. If you are first in your market, you can make the market unappealing to rivals if you and your investors are willing to price low and accept a modest profit margin. Faced with modest profits, would-be competitors are likely to stay away.

- Continually refresh your offer to customers. Think of all the ways you can make your product more appealing: by adding new features or color choices, lowering the price, making it more convenient to purchase, eliminating quality problems, or providing amazing customer service.

Such initiatives can create barriers to competition or make you the vendor of choice in a crowded field. Together, they will help you sustain growth.

Expanding into Other Markets

Does your venture have unique advantages that make it possible to move successfully into other markets? If it does, you can keep growth churning. Other markets may be geographic regions where you currently have no distribution. Assuming that customer needs in those unserved regions are the same or similar to those you are currently satisfying, geographic expansion is the answer—either through your own sales and marketing efforts or indirectly through distributors or a sales representation arrangement.

Other untapped markets may be found within your current geographic range. Here a few ideas for doing so:

- Find new uses for the same product. For example, almost every household has a small box of baking soda (sodium bicarbonate) in the kitchen. Most families will not use more than one box per year for cooking. One of the leading suppliers aimed to change this. Its advertising campaign encouraged people to put an open box of its baking soda in the refrigerator to absorb food odors. And, of course, it recommended changing that box every month. Mixing baking soda in the cat's litter box was yet another sales-generating idea. This campaign greatly increased sales to existing customers and created many new ones.

- Find ways to alter or customize your product to the needs of other niches. For example, the Swiss manufacturer of Swatch watches learned to develop dozens of unique watches—for men, woman, teenagers, sports fans, and other groups—using the very same internal timepiece elements. The only thing that changed was the exterior case design. But that single change made it possible to exploit different market niches at very low cost.

What plan does your enterprise have for recharging the growth engine? A steady stream of new products can help, but new-product development is risky and expensive. As these examples indicate, sustained sales growth does not always require invention.

Scaling Up

Sales growth challenges the entrepreneurial firm's capacity to keep pace. A service venture which bases its production on employee output must keep hiring qualified people if it hopes to grow. Consider a management consulting firm. Its production is handled through professional employees. Thus, keeping the growth engine going requires hiring individuals who can sell and deliver consulting services. Only people with unique skills and experience are capable of providing these services, and some training may also be required. But capable personnel may be in short supply. The management team would have to ask itself, "Can we scale up our human assets fast enough to satisfy demand and our own expectations of growth?"

An entrepreneurial manufacturer or retailer must also scale up to meet the demands of growth. In most cases this involves substantial commitments of capital made well in advance of actual sales. For example, the manufacturer must usually plan and begin construction of production facilities a year or more before the first widget comes off the line. Doing so requires both capital and a strong conviction that customer demand will actually be there a year or more in the future. Where does your venture stand on this scaling up issue?

One antidote to the manufacturer's scaling up problem—at least in the short run—is to outsource. There are usually plenty of competent manufacturers willing to sell unused capacity. This is exactly what Jim Koch, founder of Boston Beer Company, did when he began his venture to brew and distribute Samuel Adams Boston

Lager and its various specialty beers. Koch, a sixth-generation brewer, left his management consulting job to start the company. And like most smart entrepreneurs he started small. He set up an R&D facility inside an abandoned Boston brewery, where he developed his initial recipes. The actual brewing and bottling—capital-intensive activities—were done on a contract basis under the supervision of Koch's brewmaster at a high-quality Pennsylvania brewery. Thus, the entrepreneur maintained control of the features that made his product distinctive; the contract brewery contributed what Koch lacked and scaled his output to customer demand. As Boston Beer Company's sales grew and distribution expanded around the United States, it employed similar brewery outsourcing arrangements to scale up quickly and without major capital outlays.

Tips on Outsourcing

Outsourcing can help you scale up rapidly without creating fixed assets that you cannot afford—or that would drag you down if demand were to falter. And it frees up managerial time and attention for the things that really differentiate your company. But observe these two cautions in outsourcing activities to others:

- Avoid outsourcing those activities that connect you directly with customers—such as sales, customer service, market research, and product or service development. These interfaces provide communication links between you and your constituency, enhancing your ability to learn about them, and for them to learn about you. If you outsource these links, your customers will become your outsourcing partner's customers.

- Avoid too great a dependence on any single outsource partner. Think what would happen if a manufacturing, assembly, or distribution partner were to fail or stop doing business with you. Hedge your bets by diversifying your outsource relationships.

The Management Challenge

Although sales may seem to be the greatest growth challenge to the entrepreneurial firm, organizational issues often eclipse it. The founding entrepreneur and start-up team must periodically reinvent their organization to cope with changing circumstances. As Amar Bhidé has put it, "To attain sustainability, the capabilities of the firm (as opposed to those of the entrepreneur) have to be somehow broadened and deepened. More qualified personnel have to be added, the specialization of functions increased, decision making decentralized, systems to cope with a larger and more complex organization instituted, and the employees oriented towards a common long-term purpose."[1] To accomplish this, the firm's founders must usually reinvent themselves; that is, they must change their mode of management from "doing things" themselves to doing things through other people. Many find this reinvention difficult. They fail to change, becoming liabilities to their firms.

The entrepreneur and the core team contribute important assets to the start-up firm: a common vision, technical skills, management skills, and personal energy and time. Growth puts a strain on each of these contributions:

- The vision must be inculcated in newly hired personnel.

- The technical skills that made the start-up successful become relatively less important as the need for operational skills increases.

- The founding team's management skills may not be up to the challenge of a larger organization.

- Their personal energy and time are finite, but the need for energy and time to direct and control the expanding enterprise keeps growing.

To remain relevant and effective, the entrepreneur and the management team must find new ways to operate. Harvard Business School professor Michael J. Roberts has described the modes of management available to the entrepreneur faced with rapid growth as follows: *To remain relevant & effective; find new ways 2 operate:*

- Real-time management of content

- Management of behavior

- Management of results

- Management of context[2]

The rest of this section describes these modes, per Roberts.

Managing Content

Day-2-day.

The most direct approach to getting things done is to do them yourself or to directly supervise those who do. Whether it's hiring a new employee, working out the design of a new product, or moving goods through production and into the stockroom, the content manager is intimately involved. In a start-up organization, the CEO and management team often follow this approach. And why not? The scope of activity is small and employees are few.

The content mode provides substantial control for the entrepreneur. And control appeals to entrepreneurs. Many people are, in fact, motivated to start their own companies out of an innate need or desire to control their work and future. But as operations expand, the entrepreneur's time and energy cannot keep pace. Also, his or her ability to make good decisions may falter as new challenges arise that require special skills or experience. Failing to recognize when the content mode of management is no longer appropriate can cause the business to fail.

Managing Behavior

specify how ppl should behave that lead to success & codify thru policies

In the managing behavior mode, according to Roberts, you specify how people should behave. Leaders who follow this mode identify the behaviors that lead to success and codify them through policies, rules, and procedures that employees are told to follow. Unlike the content-oriented manager, the behavior-mode founder of, say, a

monitors compliance

medical diagnostic laboratory doesn't supervise the day-to-day work of test lab workers. Instead, the founder trains them to run specific tests and then audits their compliance with that training.

This management mode can leverage the time and effort of the entrepreneur, making it possible to maintain control over a growing enterprise. Instead of trying to manage everything, the founder relies on policies, rules, procedures, job design, and behavior-auditing systems to do the heavy lifting.

This approach is most useful when subordinates are inexperienced or need clear direction. For example, the manager of a newly trained group of salespeople might tell them the following: "I want each of you to talk with twenty prospective clients every day. Do that and you should get one new account per day, or five every week. After six months you'll have a solid base of commission business." If employees agree to this work strategy, the manager can then use his or her time to monitor compliance with the twenty-contact rule, helping where needed.

Managing Results

One problem with the manage-behavior mode is that it assumes that the desired results will follow if people will only behave in prescribed ways. This doesn't always happen. In the salesperson example just given, simply talking to the required number of prospects many not produce the desired result. Worse, it assumes that the manager's prescription is the only way to produce the desired results.

But that's not always the case. In many scientific and engineering endeavors, for example, employees must solve complex problems for which there are no clear guidelines. In these cases, management must look to its talented and creative employees to find optimal solutions. The results-mode manager says, for example, "We need to design a military vehicle that is fuel-efficient (twenty-five miles per gallon on paved roads), that is capable of driving over rough terrain, and that can protect the driver and five passengers from small-arms fire." Employees are told what the result should look like and are given responsibility for producing it. Returning to our salesperson example, the manager might simply tell each employee that the annual goal is to produce a minimum of 150,000 euros in commission revenue.

Results-mode management saves time for time-strapped entrepreneurs. Instead of specifying what people in different jobs should do and how to do it, they can concentrate on providing the resources, the training, and the motivation that people need to produce results.

Managing Context

Context-mode managers also focus on results, but they seek it more broadly: by shaping the culture, values, and structure of the organization. Generally speaking, they aim to create an environment that will naturally attract and retain highly competent employees and allow them to do their best work. According to Michael Roberts, these managers use employee selection, employee development, and communications to shape the context of work. Little or no time is spent by upper management on telling people what to do or how to do it.

Is there a best mode of management? Certainly not. But there may be a best mode for a particular firm at a particular point in its development. For example, McDonald's owes a lot of its success to its highly controlled, behavior-mode style of management, which relies on procedures and job design to prepare and serve its products with high efficiency. It would never tell its crews, "Figure out the best way to handle all those customers who are lined up for our food." It has spent years developing an efficient operational blueprint. Yet the rigid, by-the-book rules that work for McDonalds would be disastrous for a creative design company such as IDEO.

So be alert to your current needs and understand how they are changing. As Roberts has written, attention to the transitions between modes is critical. "By magnifying the volume and scope of work, growth forces the manager to evolve from a particular mode to one that requires less hands-on, real-time involvement. This means moving along the content-behavior-results-context spectrum."[3]

Which management mode are you using today? Is it appropriate for your current state of development and growth? Table 9-1 is

TABLE 9-1

The Management Mode Matrix

| | MODE | | | |
	Content	Behavior	Results	Context
Situation	Young, small, simple enterprise	Somewhat larger, more involved enterprise	Large, complex organization	Very large, very complex, mature organization
Driving assumptions	Insufficient knowledge, experience to plan Subordinates not capable of independent action or decisions	Too little time to do everything Subordinates can act independently but in accordance with managerial prescription	Too little time Subordinates can achieve better outcomes with their own means	Too little time and knowledge Right people in the right environment with right mission will succeed
Behavior	On the front lines Barking orders Pitching in to help out	Developing process and procedure Observing	Attending meetings, reviews Studying plans, papers, reports Writing memos	Lots of time on key hires and promotion Tone-setting events
Key skills, tools	Action Decisions	Policies Procedures Behavior audit	Plans Budgets Organizing structure and systems	Communication Leadership by example

Source: Michael J. Roberts, "Managing Transitions in the Growing Enterprise," in *The Entrepreneurial Venture,* 2nd edition, eds. William A. Sahlman, Howard H. Stevenson, Michel J. Roberts, and Amar Bhidé (Boston: Harvard Business School Press, 1999), 390.

Michael Roberts's assessment of when the different modes are most appropriate, along with the assumptions, behaviors, and tools associated with each.

Although the four modes discussed in this section help us think conceptually about how best to manage in different circumstances, no law of nature dictates that an executive can use only one mode at any given time. For example, Bill Gates still practices content management to some degree. Although he is chairman of a huge and diverse enterprise and although he pays substantial attention to the context of Microsoft's enterprise, he still takes a hands-on approach to product development. You may find reasons to do the same. Perhaps a hands-on approach to helping a newly appointed manager succeed is compatible with a result mode of dealing with the overall operation.

Is It Time to Change the Guard?

Many entrepreneurs have demonstrated a capacity not only to launch a successful venture but also to actively guide it successfully through years of growth. Examples include Bill Gates (Microsoft), Herb Kelleher (Southwest Airlines), Scott McNealy (Sun Microsystems), Michael Dell (Dell Computer), Scott D. Cook (Intuit), Steve Jobs (Apple), and serial entrepreneur Richard Branson (Virgin Group). Each was successful at adapting his management mode to the needs of the business as it grew and changed. Not all entrepreneurs have this adaptive capacity; they either cannot change the behaviors that served them well in a small, entrepreneurial setting—and habits of behavior are very difficult to change—or they actively resist changes that would dilute their control.

In either case, the inability of the founder-leader to adapt as the enterprise becomes larger and more complex can have these damaging consequences:

- Employee initiative is smothered by the founder's insistence on controlling all activities and making all important decisions. The best employees eventually leave in frustration.

- The organization misses opportunities because it can operate only at the pace of the overworked founder.

- The scope of the enterprise is limited to the knowledge and vision of the founder.

Getting Help

At this point you should reflect on your own management capabilities and your ability and willingness to change as your business expands. Is your business at a transition point, where your style of leading and management must change? Can you adapt? Are you willing to adapt?

If you are willing to adapt but have difficulty in doing so, two practical recourses are available. The first is to surround yourself with people who can and will give you objective feedback on your management style—including criticism. These could include other members of the management team and members of your board. What you want are people who are not afraid to tell you if your grip on the business is too tight (or too loose) and where you need help. They can also tell you when it's time for you to go—that is, when it's time to bring in professional management. Feedback of this type will help you adjust to the demands of the business and will support the collaboration that every enterprise needs to succeed.

A second source of help is an executive coach. Executive coaches provide a one-on-one, customized approach to altering behavior, with the goal of improving on-the-job performance. Executive coaches, in general, follow one of two approaches. The first, which we will call diagnosis and development, is the traditional approach. It has strong roots in psychology and is deeper in its method, but it takes longer to deliver. The other, called the prescriptive approach, has more in common with the everyday coaching that managers give to their subordinates. It is faster and more direct. Each has its advantages.

Executive coaching is expensive: anywhere between $1,500 and $15,000 per day. At several visits per month over months or years, the bill can get large. But it may be worth it to you and your company.

If you cannot or will not adapt to the changing requirements of your company, it may be time to change your role or step aside. There is certainly no shame in either. Steve Jobs had the good sense to confine himself to the chairman's job, leaving the operational details to other hands. eBay's Pierre Omidyar did the same thing when he hired Meg Whitman as CEO. Lotus founder Mitch Kapor resigned and went off to find other challenges.

Stepping Aside

Some people are simply not suited to be leaders of large organizations. Either they lack managerial and interpersonal skills, or the job of business leadership is incompatible with their temperaments or deep-seated life goals. Consider this hypothetical example:

Roger is a Ph.D. molecular biologist. He has spent his entire adult life in university settings, both teaching and conducting funded research. In 1996, he developed a molecule that had potential therapeutic value for use in chickens and turkeys. Under the terms of his employment, he was free to exploit the commercial possibilities of his discovery in return for a 25 percent share claimed by his university. Thanks to his reputation, Roger received seed financing from both the university and a venture capital firm.

Roger was content in his role as CEO of the business in the early development stage. Most of his time continued to be spent in the laboratory, where he felt most at home. But as his discovery entered the testing phase and the company hired a product manager and administrative assistant, he began to feel out of his element. Approval and commercialization of the product only made Roger's life less fulfilling. He found that he was wearing his executive hat much more and his lab coat much less. Nor did he like dealing with the venture capitalists and the M.B.A.'s they virtually forced him to hire. He didn't enjoy either type of person. One night he told his wife, "Now that we've demonstrated the therapeutic value of ChickenFix, everything seems anticlimactic."

Clearly, Roger's heart isn't in his executive role. His life is dedicated to science and discovery and not to getting regulatory approval, working out manufacturing and distribution arrangements, and building a larger enterprise.

In Roger's situation and many others, the best thing for the business is to bring in professional management, with the founder staying on as chairman of the board. This is also a realistic solution when the founders are simply incapable of handling the kind of work entailed in business-building: negotiating with suppliers; sales; setting up procedures and control systems; dealing with people problems; scrambling for money; and delegating tasks. Unfortunately, many businesses do not recognize the need for professional management soon enough to avoid a crisis.

According to transition experts Eric Flamholtz and Yvonne Randle, founder-entrepreneurs find it very difficult to let go. Some try to change their behavior as a way of avoiding it, but they often fail. Others, the authors write, "merely give the illusion of turning the organization over to professional managers." Flamholtz and Randle cite the case of one founder who hired two experienced managers, made a big deal about how he was turning over the reins, "and then proceeded to turn them into 'managerial eunuchs'" by continuing to control everything.[4]

Signs That Professional Management May Be Needed

- Every decision must be made at the top.

- Policies for handling routine functions are almost nonexistent.

- The founder-leader does not delegate.

- The firm's human resources are not being developed.

- Decisions are made, but no one follows through with action.

- Accounting functions are haphazard and amateurish.

- Attempts to recruit competent people are fruitless.

- People spend too much of their time putting out fires.

Flamholtz and Randle's very useful book, *Growing Pains,* on the challenges of entrepreneurial growth, states that "developing certain systems and processes are essential if a firm is to continue to grow successfully and profitably during its life cycle."[5] Professional managers know how to develop those systems and processes, and your company will need them at some point if it continues to grow.

From the perspective of your firm today, how does professional management look? Are you at the point where a lack of systems and processes is holding it back? Are you personally up to the challenge of building the business, or would the company be better off if you stepped aside in favor of experienced managers?

Summing Up

- Growth forces companies through transitions for which the original management team may be ill prepared.

- Continued growth is usually a function of a sustainable strategy, the ability to expand into other markets, and mechanisms for scaling up the volume of output.

- Companies have several mechanisms for sustaining growth. They include (1) exploiting the learning curve to maintain a cost advantage, (2) not pricing for maximum profit (a practice that attracts competitors), and (3) continually refreshing the offer to customers.

- Scaling up to meet rising demand can often be accomplished by outsourcing peripheral tasks to suppliers. However, outsourcing core tasks—particularly those that put you in direct contact with customers—can have very bad consequences.

- Growth challenges the founding management team, whose members may lack the skills, experience, or temperament for leading a larger, more complex organization.

- The work of Michael Roberts describes four modes of management: real-time management of content; management of behavior; management of results; and management of context. The founder and management team must recognize which mode is appropriate in the circumstances and must know when to change from one to another.

- A few entrepreneurs have successfully adapted with the growth of their companies. Others must either change themselves (something that is very difficult), change their roles by bringing in professional management, or cash in their equity and move on to new challenges.

Keeping the Entrepreneurial Spirit Alive

The Ultimate Challenge of Success

Key Topics Covered in This Chapter

- *how size, served markets, and complacency sap the entrepreneurial spirit*

- *seven things that leaders can do to keep the entrepreneurial spirit alive*

PEOPLE ASSOCIATE entrepreneurial ventures with innovation. And they are usually right. A successful entrepreneur brings something new to the marketplace—a unique product or service that differentiates the company and gives it a competitive advantage. Innovation may take the form of a technical advance, such as a thin screen computer monitor with much higher performance, or a welcomed new service, such as Web-based home grocery delivery. The innovation may also be something that customers never see, such as a breakthrough manufacturing process that slashes time and cost from the manufacturing process. Henry Ford's assembly line accomplished this in the twentieth century; process innovations that make it possible to produce smaller and more complex semiconductor chips at lower cost are a modern equivalent.

Newness that customers view favorably is usually the entrepreneur's wedge for fitting into a profitable market niche. It is difficult to think of successful entrepreneurial firms that have failed the innovation test.

Established companies, in contrast, are often viewed as slow in identifying and exploiting opportunities and as too rigid to innovate. That perception contradicts evidence of innovation in some established companies. Both Honda and Toyota introduced the hybrid (electric-gasoline), super-low-emission automobile to the market—perhaps the single greatest innovation in automotive technology in half a century. This feat was not merely technical but matched a real need for substantial emissions reductions and fuel conservation.

Intel, another huge enterprise, continues to innovate on the frontiers of microprocessing, producing chips that run faster, use less power, and handle more computational work. IBM's development of the silicon germanium chip is yet another example. Similarly, 3M continues to uphold its decades-long reputation as a serial innovator.

But for every Honda, Toyota, Intel, IBM, and 3M there are dozens of large manufacturers, financial institutions, pharmaceutical companies, and service firms for which innovation is a forgotten art. When they need innovation they buy it through acquisition or licensing agreements—and usually from entrepreneurial companies.

The danger of losing the entrepreneurial spirit and the ability to innovate as their start-up companies grow should be a concern of all business founders. This chapter takes a hard look at why many small firms lose their entrepreneurial spark as they succeed and grow. It also offers practical remedies.

Three Challenges

Why are large, established firms less adept at innovation than entrepreneurial firms? There are three plausible answers: size, the desire to serve existing customers, and complacency. All are challenges that the entrepreneurial enterprise must confront and defeat as it grows.

The Size Problem

Size requires specialization of functions, creates communication and coordination problems between functions, and requires control systems—review boards and approval requirements—that often frustrate creative people and impede the pace of idea development. The problems that the founding team solved informally over coffee now require formal meetings involving many people with divergent views. The more people who are involved, the longer it takes to reach agreement on the simplest things. And agreements are more likely to be compromises than optimal solutions.

The Existing Customers Problem

Every businessperson is taught the importance of customers and the importance of serving and retaining them. Diligent serving of existing customers, however, has two innovation-impeding consequences:

1. Existing customers often discourage innovation by their vendors. For example, a major technical advance in computing can jeopardize the investments customers have made in existing hardware, software, and training. Consequently, these customers often urge vendors to continue supplying them with parts and upgrades—in effect, to stay in their old businesses. Some call this phenomenon the "tyranny of served markets." Companies that slavishly give customers what they want concentrate on incremental innovations to existing products, leaving the invention of truly breakthrough products to rivals. Eventually, these same customers will abandon their vendors and switch their business to the innovative rivals.

2. Management shifts its focus to operations. The job of serving customers profitably requires operational excellence. As the business grows, management's attention is increasingly absorbed by people issues, marketing, finance, production, logistics, customer service, and so forth. Innovation can easily slip off the radar.

Complacency

The success that propels growth creates a powerful impulse toward complacency and self-satisfaction. It tricks people into believing that if they simply continue doing what they are doing, all will be well. Author and scholar Richard Pascle described this phenomenon many years ago as the paradox of success. Success, in his view, plants the seeds of eventual failure.

When faced with a new competing technology, for example, the impulse of many successful companies is to invest still further in the technology that made them successful in the first place. This was observed when steam ships challenged makers of sailing ships, when Edison's electric lighting systems challenged the gas illumination companies in the late 1800s, and when jet engines challenged piston-driven aircraft engines in the late 1940s. The established companies threatened by these innovations continued to invest in and marginally improve their mature technologies even as the new ones were becoming better and cheaper by the month.

The newly launched entrepreneurial firm is untroubled by the problems of size, the tyranny of served markets, and complacency. Success and growth, however, have a way of undermining that advantage. Sales growth must be supported by organizational infrastructure and control systems, and the entrepreneur's innovative spirit is gradually dissipated. The challenge to the founding team, then, is to keep the innovative spirit alive as the organization grows and serves more customers.

The Characteristics of Innovative Companies

In his classic article "Tough-Minded Ways to Get Innovative," Harvard emeritus professor Andrall Pearson, a former managing director of McKinsey & Company, identified two distinguishing characteristics of competitive companies. "First, they understand that consistent innovation is the key to a company's survival," he wrote. "Being innovative some of the time, in one or two areas, just won't work. Second, they know that the most powerful changes they can make are those that create value for their existing and potential customers." These companies, in his view, are always seeking ways to make their businesses more appealing to customers.

Does your firm have these characteristics? Is it losing them as it grows larger?

SOURCE: Andrall E. Pearson, "Tough-Minded Ways to Get Innovative," *Harvard Business Review,* May–June 1988, 99–106.

What Entrepreneurial Leaders Must Do

Fortunately, success and growth are not incompatible with the entrepreneurial spirit, as the examples provided earlier confirm. But what can the leadership do to ensure the continued vitality of that spirit? This section contains some practical advice for staying aggressive, innovative, and responsive to market conditions.

Preserve an Innovation–Friendly Culture

The impact of organizational culture on creativity and idea generation is well understood. In the absence of a supportive culture, creativity and innovation will not germinate and grow.

Authors Michael Tushman and Charles O'Reilly point to pre-Gerstner IBM as a culture in which innovation fell on infertile soil. It was, in their words, "a culture characterized by an inward focus, extensive procedures for resolving issues through consensus and 'push back,' arrogance bred by previous success, and a sense of entitlement on the part of some employees that guaranteed jobs without a quid pro quo."[1] If your company's culture is taking on these characteristics, then creativity and innovation are unlikely to flourish. Worse, the most innovative people will become discouraged and dispirited, and they will look elsewhere for work.

These questions will help you determine whether your company is losing its creative edge:

- Is our current success making us self-satisfied and complacent?

- Are we inwardly focused?

- Do we punish risk takers who fail?

- Are creative people and new ideas unwelcome or unappreciated in this company?

- Do we fail to reward acts of creativity?

- Are we bureaucratic in the way we handle new ideas?

- Are hierarchy and its symbols creeping into our culture?

If you answered yes to any one of these questions, a serious evaluation and adjustment to your organizational culture are in order.

Establish Strategic Direction

If innovative people lose sight of where the company should be heading, they are likely to generate and pursue ideas that don't fit, that eat up resources, and that eventually will be rejected before commercialization. That costs money and dissipates the energy of idea generators.

Because both creative energy and money are scarce commodities, it makes sense to encourage idea generation within boundaries defined by company strategy. For example, if your company is a direct mail apparel merchandiser, encourage ideas that fall within the boundaries of "better linkages with our customers" and "fast and accurate order fulfillment." Within those strategy-related boundaries, new ideas for improving customer intelligence, order processing, and logistics should be welcomed. If you set the boundaries right, your company's creative energies will naturally focus themselves in areas with the greatest payoff potential.

Be Personally Involved with Innovation

As your entrepreneurial firm grows, operational issues will begin to eat up your time. This is natural. But don't allow operational humdrum to detach you from the innovation on which your future depends. Some of the best and most successful executives have been happiest and most effective when they were in the R&D lab rubbing elbows with bench scientists and technicians. Bill Hewlett, David Packard, and Motorola's Bob Galvin fit this description. So does Bill Gates today. Leaders cannot make good decisions about R&D if they operate in a vacuum or think of innovation as a mysterious force. They must understand the technical issues facing their organizations and the portfolio of ideas and projects that are in the pipeline at any given time. Hewlett, Packard, Galvin, and Gates all did this.

So stay very close to sources of innovation within your company as it grows. Visit the research people regularly. Have lunch with project teams. Get to know key people one-on-one. Understand the technical hurdles that stand between appealing ideas and their commercialization. Staying close to innovative activities has several beneficial effects:

- It sends a powerful signal to employees that innovation matters.

- It provides entrepreneurial leaders with opportunities to articulate the strategic direction of the enterprise and the boundaries within which innovation should be pursued.

- It keeps leaders up-to-date on technical and market issues.

Continually Improve the Idea–to–Commercialization Process

Chances are that the innovative idea that spawned your company was conceived and developed in an informal way. You didn't have stage-gate committees and approval processes to deal with. The growth that follows success, however, makes such processes both necessary and useful. Indeed, companies that continue to innovate and grow have a process for generating ideas, recognizing which of them have commercial potential, and evaluating those promising ideas, followed by development and commercialization (see figure 10-1). You will need

FIGURE 10-1

The Innovation Process

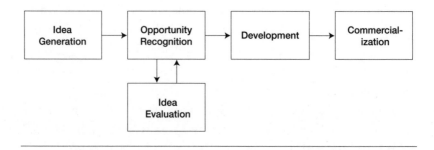

such a process, too; otherwise your innovative efforts will be ad hoc, arbitrary, and a waste of resources. A good process does the following:

- Generates a sufficient number of good ideas

- Is free of the bottlenecks that impede development and frustrate innovators

- Is free of politics

- Encourages calculated risk taking

- Is not arbitrary

- Creates cheap failures

- Channels resources to the worthiest projects

- Involves people who understand the company's capabilities, its strategy, and its customers

Like the shaping of organizational culture, developing and improving the innovation process are jobs for founders and the management team. And it's one of the most important jobs they will ever handle.

Apply Portfolio Thinking

Many entrepreneurial firms, particularly in high-tech, are launched with only one or two development projects in process. That makes organizational life simple: All resources, brainstorming, and marketing can be concentrated on those one or two things. As these firms succeed and grow, however, they may have dozens of funded projects in play at any given time. Some may be low-risk, short-term projects that aim to incrementally improve an existing product. Others may represent radically new concepts that aim to create new markets. Still others may fall between these two extremes.

Because incremental and radical projects entail substantial differences in risk levels, time frames, and potential payoffs, management must employ portfolio thinking in dealing with them. Portfolio

Portfolio

thinking helps managers see a set of ongoing projects in terms of risk/return characteristics. And when they understand those characteristics, they can shape and manage the portfolio to achieve the right balance of risk and potential return.

As a first step toward portfolio thinking, it is often helpful to "map" ongoing projects onto a two-dimensional matrix like the one in figure 10-2. Here, the horizontal axis indicates the maturity or newness of market or technology factors. The vertical axis indicates rising levels of technical challenge, uncertainty, and economic opportunity. Each circle in the matrix represents a project, and the size of each circle indicates the magnitude of resources currently dedicated to it.

FIGURE 10-2

Innovation Portfolio Matrix

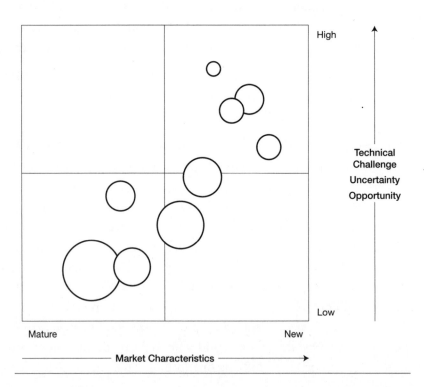

In the matrix shown here, the biggest projects are cautious. They have mature technical and market characteristics. As a result, these projects are among the least technically challenging and involve the least risk and potential opportunity for the company. In contrast, the small projects in the upper-right quadrant involve higher technical risk and address new markets, but they also hold the prospect for greater economic opportunity for the company.

Tips for Making Good Decisions

Keeping the entrepreneurial spirit alive means continually pushing into uncharted terrain with R&D projects, market initiatives, and human resource investments. Each involves making decisions under conditions of uncertainty. And good decisions are essential. Here are a few tips that can help you make those decisions:

• Exclude friends and yes-men from your management team and board of directors. You need solid advice as you consider investments in an innovative idea.

• Surround yourself with people who have complementary skills and different approaches to analyzing issues and making decisions. Listen to their suggestions and arguments, even when you disagree. These other voices can help you avoid walking off a cliff.

• Learn when to cut your losses. You cannot win the game if you don't play. But don't play every game to the end. Like a good poker player, recognize when you're pouring resources into a losing hand, and have the courage to walk away with your losses.

• Double-check assumptions. What looks rosy can be a disaster if those assumptions are not realistic.

Try constructing a similar matrix for your company. When you've mapped out your current projects, what does it tell you? If most projects and resources are located in the lower-left quadrant, your company is being very risk averse and may be doing too little to address future opportunities, new technologies, and new markets. On the other hand, if most projects and resources are in the upper-right quadrant, it is being very aggressive, perhaps dangerously so.

What would constitute a suitable risk/reward balance for your company? As the entrepreneurial leader, can you articulate that balance to your employees and investors?

Hire People Who Have Entrepreneurial Attitudes

The most important decisions an entrepreneur makes as the company grows involve hiring. Growth creates a need for new people, but what types of people are most suitable?

When hiring new-product developers, executives should look for people who have a balance of strong technical background and an appreciation for the larger concerns of the organization. Specifically, they should have (1) a good feel for the trajectories of technologies important to the company and (2) a genuine curiosity about the stated and latent needs of customers. People who are narrowly interested in applying their technical skills will rarely produce the practical innovations you need.

New hires in general should

- be comfortable with change

- view unmet needs as opportunities

- adopt appropriate time horizons

- enjoy collaborative work

- think and act like entrepreneurs

People being hired as supervisors or managers should be comfortable with the idea of participative management. Anything else will lead to the kind of hierarchical, bureaucratic environment that kills the entrepreneurial spirit. If you do nothing else, give no quarter to hierarchy and bureaucracy.

Create an Ambidextrous Organization

Leaders of fast-growing entrepreneurial companies quickly find themselves being tugged in two directions. On the one hand, they must focus on the innovations required to sustain growth. On the other, they must run an operationally effective organization. How can they possibly do both?

Authors Michael Tushman and Charles O'Reilly suggest that leaders create "ambidextrous" organizations—that is, organizations that can "get today's work done more effectively and [also] anticipate tomorrow's discontinuities."[2] These are seemingly contradictory capabilities, but enterprises that have them are capable of excelling in the present even as they create the future.

The source of the challenge is not hard to understand. Success in the current business is usually driven by certainty, efficiency, and cost control. The future business, on the other hand, is the product of an innovation process that is uncertain, inefficient, and costly. Not many executives can operate successfully in these two very different worlds. Most become absorbed with one to the detriment of the other. In most cases, the immediate problems of the business dominate their time and attention, leaving the future business to be treated as a stepchild.

The antidote, per Tushman and O'Reilly, is an ambidextrous organization. Here are a few suggestions for developing one:

1. Assess where you are in terms of innovation trends. Are your current products and technologies in the early phase of perfection, or are they mature? Do new technologies have the potential to undermine your business?

2. Assess your company's operations. Are they effective, fast, and efficient? Are major cost improvements possible?

3. Based on your answers to steps 1 and 2, reorder your priorities and resources. You need to be very good at both current operations and innovation.

Summing Up

- Growth challenges the entrepreneurial spirit. Size creates specialization of functions, communication problems, and control systems that frustrate creativity and idea development.

- Once a company has customers, the "tyranny of served markets" can block a company's capacity to innovate.

- The success that accompanies growth often leads to complacency, which is antithetical to the entrepreneurial spirit.

- Establish the strategic direction within which innovation should take place.

- Entrepreneurial leaders can keep the spirit alive if they (1) preserve an innovation-friendly culture, (2) establish a strategic direction, (3) remain personally involved with innovation, (4) continually improve the idea-to-commercialization process, (5) apply portfolio thinking to their innovative efforts, (6) hire people with entrepreneurial attitudes, and (7) create an ambidextrous organization that is effective at both getting today's work done (operations) and anticipating the future.

Harvest Time

Reaping What You've Sown

Key Topics Covered in This Chapter

- *three reasons for cashing out*

- *the advantages and shortcomings of various harvesting mechanisms*

- *methods for valuing the entrepreneur's investment*

SOME ENTREPRENEURS pass on their businesses to family members. The majority, however, eventually look for an opportunity to harvest the monetary value they have created—value that is locked up in the enterprise. This chapter examines the motivations that lead to harvesting, the primary mechanisms for doing so, and the methods used to determine business value.

Why Entrepreneurs Cash Out

There are probably as many reasons for harvesting an investment as there are entrepreneurs. Retirement is one reason. An offer "too good to refuse" is yet another. Most investment harvesting, however, tends to be motivated by one or another of the following:

- A need to diversify wealth. Successful entrepreneurs can easily get into a position where most of their wealth is dangerously concentrated in one basket. Their net worth could easily be wiped out by a change in technology, the emergence of powerful competitors, or some other business setback. Harvesting gives the entrepreneur an opportunity to diversify personal wealth.

- The business has reached the end of its line. Some successful entrepreneurs sense where the wind is blowing, and sometimes they sense an ill wind. More specifically, they realize that their business has gone about as far as it can go, at least under their leadership. They recognize that continued growth would require a new level of investment that they are not interested in making. In other cases, they can feel the competitive environment turning against them, as when the owner of several hardware stores finds that the business must now go head-to-head with a national chain having enormous buying power.

- The owner's urge to begin anew. Some entrepreneurs are motivated by the challenge of creating something out of almost nothing. They love the early phase of business-building. But when operational concerns begin to absorb most of their time, they are happy to move on. (See the "Serial Entrepreneurs" box.)

Serial Entrepreneurs

A story in the *New York Times* in December 2003 described the career of Howard Yellen, who started his first company in 1988. Between then and late 2003, Yellen, then 43, had started six companies in unrelated industries. Two had been sold (one for an undisclosed price, the other for $10 million); the others had been closed down. As described in the story, "Mr. Yellen is one of a special breed of small-business owners—the serial entrepreneur. Serial entrepreneurs thrive on the high-pressure excitement of starting a business from scratch, but invariably, whether they stick with the business for one year or ten, they depart, only to start another."

Serial entrepreneurship is not confined to small operators such as Yellen. According to the *Times* story, approximately 43 percent of chief executives of *Inc. Magazine* 500 companies anticipate starting another company in the future. Harvesting, of course, is an enabler of the serial entrepreneur. The gains from one successful venture are often sufficient to get the next two off the ground.

SOURCE: Anne Field, "Bouncing from Start-Up to Start-Up, and Loving It," *New York Times*, 11 December 2003, C6.

Harvesting Mechanisms

When a business owner has made the decision to cash out, the next step is to determine which harvesting method is most timely and appropriate. This section examines the most common of those methods as well as their advantages and shortcomings.

IPO

The role of the initial public offering in harvesting entrepreneurial investments was described earlier. When a public market for a firm's shares has been established, its founders as well as its private investors can, within certain regulatory restrictions, sell some or all of their shares. Those restrictions, however, may hold up share sales by insiders for some period and may put a cap on the number of shares that the holder of restricted shares can sell in any one-month period (SEC Rule 144). For information on SEC Rule 144, see appendix E.

The investment banker underwriting the deal will also require key pre-IPO shareholders to sign a lockup agreement barring them from selling their shares during a specified period after the company goes public. This lockup, which may last as long as six months, ensures that insiders will not dump their shares onto the market, causing losses for the public investors who stepped forward to buy shares of the IPO.

Few firms ever qualify for an IPO in any case; they are either too small or too limited in their potential, or they are in a moribund industry that doesn't attract investor interest. Even those that qualify have plenty of reasons to avoid the harvesting IPO route: deal-making costs, public scrutiny of the firm's operations, reporting requirements, and so forth. These reasons may not trouble private investors (e.g., venture capitalists); their primary interest is often to quickly cash out, lock in a high rate of return, and move on to the next opportunity.

Perhaps the best case for harvesting via an IPO is the higher price that is often obtained through this means than through others. A private study of venture capital returns during 1970 through 1982, for example, found that the gains realized through IPOs were almost *five times* as great as the next most profitable methods (acquisitions and company buybacks).[1] The IPO edge is particularly potent when investor appetite for new shares is high, if not driven by "irrational exuberance," as U.S. Federal Reserve Chairman Alan Greenspan famously described the dot-com bubble. The valuations placed on profitless dot-com companies during that period bordered on lunacy, much to the benefit of company founders and venture capitalists who managed to unload their shares before the bubble burst. Companies that went public during that giddy time yielded greater harvests than their founders and venture capitalists had any right to expect.

The dot-com era, however, was an aberration. Opportunities to reap huge harvests through IPOs occur infrequently and seldom produce the valuations seen in the late 1990s. Investor interest in IPOs is usually so cautious that founders and VCs must sit tight, work at building cash flow, and hope for a better tomorrow.

Acquisitions

Many more harvests are accomplished through mergers and acquisitions than through IPOs. Each year thousands of companies join with others in some form of strategic merger. Perhaps as many are snapped up by other companies that seek to capture their patents, product lines, manufacturing capabilities, or something else.

Mergers and acquisitions are complex transactions, and because the typical entrepreneur has no experience with them, he or she should enlist experienced legal and financial advisers to help with any proposed deal. They are particularly complex when neither of the participants is a public company whose share value can be determined from actual public trading. In these cases, valuations must be conducted.

In general, the selling entrepreneur should give careful attention to these three issues:

- **How the deal is valued.** Different valuation methods produce different results.

- **How payment will be structured.** Payment may be in the form of cash, some mix of cash and the stock of the acquiring company, or debt. In a merger the entrepreneur may end up with the stock of a newly formed company. Cash is the ideal form of payment because all other forms tie up the entrepreneur's capital in the other company for some period. But not all stock-in-payment deals are bad. For example, Sabeer Bhatia received 2.7 million shares of Microsoft when he sold his company, Hotmail, to the software giant. The shares of other acquiring companies may be less solid.

- **The relationship of the selling entrepreneur and the merged or acquired company.** Many deals provide for some period of managerial involvement by the seller. The seller may even welcome this arrangement. Approach these arrangements with care, however, because the acquirer is unlikely to give you the free hand you enjoyed in running the business that was once yours.

ESOP

An ESOP is another harvesting option for a company that lacks a public market for its shares. An ESOP (*employee stock ownership plan*) is a formal plan under which corporate shares are acquired by the plan on behalf of employees, for whom it is a tax-qualified retirement plan. In effect, the ESOP acts as a market for the owner's shares, purchasing those shares gradually over a period of years. Consider this hypothetical example:

> *Macmillan Metal Works was a closely held corporation with eighty full-time employees. Howard Macmillan, the founder, owned all the shares. Most of his family's wealth was tied up in the company, and Howard had few means of getting it out other than selling the enterprise. Howard learned from his attorney that an ESOP could meet several of his goals at once: provide a retirement plan for his employees, give employees an ownership interest in the business, and allow him to gradually cash out his shares.*
>
> *The attorney set up a plan, and Howard hired a business appraiser to develop a valuation for company shares. Based on that valuation, he sold two thousand shares that year to the plan. Qualified employees*

were then committed to purchasing specified numbers of shares each year, with Macmillan Metal Works contributing part of the purchase price. The sales proceeds, of course, went to Howard Macmillan, who used the cash to diversify his investment assets.

The ESOP harvest approach has disadvantages. One is that company shares must be valued through an independent business appraisal every year, a process that can be costly for a small company.

Shearing Versus Selling

We think of selling as a way for the entrepreneur to get a substantial amount of capital out of the enterprise. Selling is particularly important when the owner or owners want to walk away and do something else with their lives. For many owners, however, walking away isn't the issue; nor is getting all their capital out at once a primary goal. Some owners are content to periodically withdraw some of their capital to improve their living standards, to gain retirement income, or to diversify. One way to achieve this end is to pocket whatever cash flow is not needed to maintain or expand the business.

Successful ventures generate more cash flow than the amount they need to maintain a steady state condition. Growth-oriented owners reinvest that excess cash in the business: to expand the sales force, to acquire or develop new product lines, to open new retail locations, and so forth. The owner who wants to liquefy some of his capital can simply pocket this excess cash instead of reinvesting it. This "shearing" of company cash flow will limit the firm's ability to finance continued growth through internally generated cash. But for some owners, growth may no longer matter; their companies may be as large as they can comfortably handle. Those who want continued growth may find it possible to substitute debt capital for internally generated cash flow. In these cases, the owners will get part of their equity capital, and the firms will experience a change in their debt-to-equity ratios.

Another is that the employee members of the plan will one day own a majority of the shares, something that the entrepreneur may not like.

The other disadvantage involves the employees themselves. ESOPs are not always a good thing for them. Tying up part or all of their retirement funds in the shares of a single company (their employer) puts them in a doubly nondiversified position. A serious setback for the company could result in both a loss of employment and a loss of retirement fund value. The huge personal losses suffered by employees of Enron Corporation are an example of what can happen when employees have both their net worth and their current income tied up in a single enterprise.

Selling to Management

Senior managers represent another potential set of buyers for the entrepreneur seeking to harvest the investment. These senior managers understand the company and the industry. They know the cash-generating potential of the business as well as anyone. So it is not surprising when an employee group offers to buy the company from the founding owner. These cases are often referred to as management buyouts.

In many cases, the buyer group can use the assets of the company as collateral for loans they need to finance the purchase. After the purchase is made, the buyers find themselves with a very high debt-to-equity ratio—in some cases 10:1—and staggeringly large interest payments. Typically, management responds by selling operating units of the entity that are either underperforming or that don't fit their new strategy. Managers also sell the corporate aircraft and nonessential property. The cash from these sales is used immediately to pay down large chunks of the debt. At the same time, the new owners increase the amount of free cash by reducing employee headcounts, cutting expenses, and reducing inventories.

This type of transaction is called a leverage buyout (LBO), an approach that was practiced widely during the 1980s, often by outside "raiders" who recognized that the separate parts of a company could be sold for much more than the company's total market value.

Most of the LBO deals of the 1980s relied on substantial outside debt capital in the form of high-yield, or junk, bonds, an approach that is seldom available to today's buyer groups. The result is that the selling owner may have to act as lender, taking a collateral-backed note in payment for his or her share of the company. The owner's harvest in these cases is spread out over many years of principal and interest payments by the buying group.

Although they get much less press these days, LBOs still accounted for $14.5 billion in U.S. company sales transactions in the first quarter of 2003 alone. In general, the best candidates for LBOs are companies with high levels of predictable free cash flow, few requirements for capital spending, little debt, and substantial nonessential assets.

Timing Matters

No matter which method of harvesting is used, proper timing is a key element in any harvest strategy. The only exception to the strategies mentioned here is the ESOP, which features the sale of stock over many years, in both good times and bad.

As stated earlier, the window of opportunity for launching a successful IPO is narrow. For example, very few companies were able to stage an IPO during the 2000–2004 doldrums. Some industries, such as biotech, found the window shut tight.

What applies to the IPO market applies also to other forms of harvesting. The mood of investors—and business buyers—is like a pendulum that swings between optimism and fear. Buyers who are giddy with optimism will pay much more for a business than they will during periods of fear. Thus, the entrepreneur who seeks to maximize return should be alert to the mood of investors in timing the sale of shares or of the entire business.

What's It Worth?

With the exception of the shearing method, valuation is at the heart of each of the harvesting mechanisms described in this chapter.

Valuation attempts to answer a fundamental question: "What is this company really worth?" If you cannot answer that question, you will be in a poor position to negotiate a deal.

IPO Values

Share value in an IPO is generally a function of what the market-place of investors will accept and what the future of the company appears to hold. Thus, the deal's underwriter will look at the mood of investors, the price of comparable public corporate shares relative to earnings, the company's current and anticipated financial perfor-mance, proprietary technology, and growth potential. Based on this less-than-scientific process, the underwriter will suggest an issuing price per share, one that is slightly discounted to the anticipated trading level of the shares. That discount is meant to put initial in-vestors in a profitable position when trading begins.

More Rigorous Methods

Other harvesting mechanisms rely on more rigorous valuation methods. Although appendix C explains these methods and their strengths and weaknesses in some detail, it's worth mentioning them here as well. The two most reliable valuation approaches are the earnings–based method and the discounted cash flow method.

EARNINGS-BASED VALUATION. The earnings–based method multiplies one or another earnings figure from the income statement by some number. For example, a valuation specialist might find that similar companies in the same industry are selling at roughly five times earnings before interest and taxes (EBIT).

A more exacting approach adds back any depreciation or amor-tization charges that reduced income statement earnings, because those are noncash expenses. That more exacting figure is called EBITDA (earnings before interest and taxes *plus* depreciation and amortization).

The idea in both cases is to attach the multiple to the cash flows actually available to the owner. Thus, if EBIT for an entrepreneurial firm were $2 million and if similar companies in the industry were selling for five times that multiple, the value of the firm would be $10 million.

The "multiple" used in these valuations shouldn't appear from outer space. Rather, it should correspond with what other investors have paid recently for the EBIT of comparable companies that were on the sales block. So be very careful about the multiple you use, because it can make a huge difference in the estimated value of your company. You should also appreciate the fact that multiples, as with price-earnings ratios for company stock, float up and down with the moods and expectations of investors. When an industry is out of favor and when investors are pessimistic about future prospects, its multiple will slide downward. The opposite happens when an industry is in favor or when prospects for earnings growth are favorable. The lesson to the selling entrepreneur is to sell when investors are giddy with optimism.

DISCOUNTED CASH FLOW (DCF) VALUATION. The key drawback of this multiple-of-earnings method is that it is not forward-looking. It bases value on current earnings and not on what earnings will be in the future. Thus, a firm with rapidly growing earnings would probably be shortchanged by this type of valuation.

The remedy is to consider the firm's value in terms of its stream of future cash flows. It is that stream of future earnings, after all, that investors are buying. As described by Tom Copeland, Tim Koller, and Jack Murrin, authors of what many consider the bible of valuation, "The DCF approach captures all the elements that affect the value of the company in a comprehensive yet straightforward manner."[2]

The DCF valuation method requires a forecast of cash flows extending several years into the future and the application of time-value-of-money calculations. It discounts those cash flows to their present value. Professional help is usually needed to implement these requirements.

Working with a Business Appraiser

Business valuation isn't an area where the entrepreneur is likely to have either expertise or experience. Nor is it an issue that matters more than once or a few times during a business career. Nevertheless, its impact on the outcome of harvesting is huge. This suggests that the entrepreneur should learn as much as possible about this technical field—or at least enough to work with a professional business appraiser and make intelligent decisions.

Summing Up

- Entrepreneurs seek to harvest their investments for several reasons. Key among them are to diversify their wealth, to take the business to a higher level, or to try something new.

- Although it is available to very few enterprises, an IPO can give the entrepreneurial team liquidity over time.

- For most companies, selling the company through an acquisition is a more likely harvesting mechanism than is an IPO. Here, the entrepreneurs should pay close attention to how the deal is valued, how payment will be structured (cash, stock, debt), and how any ongoing relationship with the acquiring entity or merger partner will be defined.

- An ESOP is a tax-qualified retirement plan that purchases owner shares over a period of years. In effect, the owner sells to the employees.

- In many cases the management group will join together to buy out the founder-owner. This can be achieved through a leverage buyout or through a debt arrangement with the seller.

- One popular approach to business valuation multiplies earnings before interest and taxes (EBIT) times a number called a multiple. The multiple should correspond with what other investors have paid recently for the EBIT of comparable companies.

- The discounted cash flow (DCF) approach to valuation provides a better measure of company value because it is future oriented.

Understanding Financial Statements

A Primer

What does your company own, and what does it owe to others? What are its sources of revenue, and how has it spent its money? How much profit has it made? What is the state of your company's financial health? This appendix helps you answer those questions by explaining the three essential financial statements: the balance sheet, the income statement, and the cash flow statement. The appendix also helps you understand some of the managerial issues implicit in these statements and broadens your financial know-how through discussion of two important concepts: financial leverage and the financial structure of the firm.

If you have a business degree or senior management experience, you may already know as much as you need to know about these topics. But many entrepreneurs have neither. For example, Ken Olsen, the legendary founder of Digital Equipment Corporation in the late 1950s, knew all about electrical engineering and programming, and he had terrific ideas for building a new generation of computers. But he knew next to nothing about financial statements, which the venture capitalists wanted him to include in his business plan. According to entrepreneurial lore, Olsen went to the public library, borrowed a copy of Paul Samuelson's famous economics textbook, found an example of a balance sheet and income statement, and used them as models for his projected figures. The venture capitalists were impressed and gave him the money he needed to develop his business.

If you're already knowledgeable about financial statements, you can probably skip this appendix. But if you're more like novice entrepreneur Ken Olsen (and we hope you are, since he made lots of money and accomplished great things), then continue reading. The ability to read and interpret financial statements is essential for the enterprising businessperson. When the conversation turns to "current liabilities," "profit margin," and "working capital," the meaning of these terms must be understood.

Why Financial Statements?

Financial statements are the essential documents of business. Managers use them to assess performance and identify areas in which intervention is required. Shareholders use them to keep tabs on how well their capital is being managed. Outside investors use them to identify opportunities. And lenders and suppliers routinely examine financial statements to determine the creditworthiness of the companies with which they deal.

Publicly traded companies are required by the Securities and Exchange Commission (SEC) to produce financial statements and make them available to everyone as part of the full-disclosure requirement the SEC places on publicly owned and traded companies. Companies not publicly traded are under no such requirement, but their private owners and bankers expect financial statements nevertheless.

Financial statements—the balance sheet, the income statement, and the cash flow statement—follow the same general format from company to company. And even though specific line items may vary with the nature of a company's business, the statements are usually similar enough to allow you to compare one business's performance against another's.

The Balance Sheet

Many people go to a doctor once a year to get a checkup—a snapshot of their physical well-being at a particular time. Similarly, companies prepare balance sheets as a way of summarizing their financial positions at a given point in time, usually at the end of the month, the quarter, or the fiscal year.

In effect, the balance sheet describes the assets controlled by the business and shows how those assets are financed—with the funds of creditors (liabilities), with the capital of the owners, or with both. A balance sheet reflects the following basic accounting equation:

Assets = Liabilities + Owners' Equity

Assets in this equation are the things in which a company invests so that it can conduct business. Examples include cash and financial instruments, inventories of raw materials and finished goods, land, buildings, and equipment. Assets also include money owed to the company by customers and others—an asset category referred to as *accounts receivable*.

Now look at the other side of the equation, starting with liabilities. To acquire its necessary assets, a company often borrows money or promises to pay suppliers for various goods and services. Moneys owed to creditors are called *liabilities*. For example, a computer company may acquire $1 million worth of motherboards from an electronic parts supplier, with payment due in thirty days. In doing so, the computer company increases its inventory assets by $1 million and increases its liabilities—in the form of *accounts payable*—by an equal amount. The equation stays in balance. Similarly, if the same company were to borrow $100,000 from a bank, the cash infusion would increase its assets by $100,000 and its liabilities by the same amount.

Owners' equity, also known as shareholders' or stockholders' equity, is what is left after total liabilities are deducted from total assets. Thus, a company that has $3 million in total assets and $2 million in liabilities would have owners' equity of $1 million.

Assets − Liabilities = Owners' Equity
$3,000,000 − $2,000,000 = $1,000,000

If $500,000 of this same company's uninsured assets burned up in a fire, its liabilities would remain the same, but its owners'

equity—what's left after all claims against assets are satisfied—would
be reduced to $500,000:

Assets – Liabilities = Owners' Equity
$2,500,000 – $2,000,000 = $500,000

Thus, the balance sheet "balances" a company's assets and liabilities. Notice, for example, that the total assets equal total liabilities
and owners' equity in the balance sheet of Amalgamated Hat Rack,
our sample company (table A-1). The balance sheet also describes
how much the company has invested in assets and shows where the
money is invested. Further, the balance sheet indicates how much of
those monetary investments in assets comes from creditors (liabilities) and how much comes from owners (equity). Analysis of the balance sheet can give you an idea of how efficiently a company is using
its assets and how well it is managing its liabilities.

Balance sheet data is most helpful when compared with the same
information from one or more previous years. Consider the balance
sheet of Amalgamated Hat Rack. First, this statement represents the
company's financial position at a moment in time: December 31,
2002. A comparison of the figures for 2001 against those for 2002
shows that Amalgamated is moving in a positive direction: It has increased its owner's equity by $100,000.

Assets

You should understand some details about this particular financial
statement. The balance sheet begins by listing the assets most easily
converted to cash: cash on hand and marketable securities, receivables, and inventory. These are called *current assets*. Generally, current
assets are those that can be converted into cash within one year.

Next, the balance sheet tallies other assets that are tougher to
convert to cash—for example, buildings and equipment. These are
called plant assets or, more commonly, *fixed assets* (because it is hard
to change them into cash).

Because most fixed assets, except land, depreciate—or become
less valuable—over time, the company must reduce the stated value of

TABLE A-1

Amalgamated Hat Rack Balance Sheet as of December 31, 2002

	2002	2001	Increase (Decrease)
Assets			
Cash and marketable securities	$355,000	$430,000	$(75,000)
Accounts receivable	$555,000	$512,000	$43,000
Inventory	$835,000	$755,000	$80,000
Prepaid expenses	$123,000	$98,000	$25,000
Total current assets	$1,868,000	$1,795,000	$73,000
Gross property, plant, and equipment	$2,100,000	$1,900,000	$200,000
Less: accumulated depreciation	$333,000	$234,000	$99,000
Net property, plant, and equipment	$1,767,000	$1,666,000	$101,000
Total assets	$3,635,000	$3,461,000	$174,000
Liabilities and Owner's Equity			
Accounts payable	$450,000	$430,000	$20,000
Accrued expenses	$98,000	$77,000	$21,000
Income tax payable	$17,000	$9,000	$8,000
Short-term debt	$435,000	$500,000	$65,000
Total current liabilities	$1,000,000	$1,016,000	$(16,000)
Long-term debt	$750,000	$660,000	$90,000
Total liabilities	$1,750,000	$1,676,000	$74,000
Contributed capital	$900,000	$850,000	$50,000
Retained earnings	$985,000	$935,000	$50,000
Total owner's equity	$1,885,000	$1,785,000	$100,000
Total liabilities and owner's equity	$3,635,000	$3,461,000	$174,000

Source: HMM Finance.

these fixed assets by something called accumulated depreciation. Gross property, plant, and equipment minus accumulated depreciation equals the current book value of property, plant, and equipment.

Some companies list *goodwill* among their assets. If a company has purchased another company for a price above the fair market value of its assets, that so-called goodwill is recorded as an asset. This is, however, strictly an accounting fiction. Goodwill may also represent intangible things such as brand names or the acquired company's excellent reputation. These may have real value. So too can other intangible assets, such as patents.

Finally, we come to the last line of the asset section of the balance sheet: total assets. Total assets represents the sum of current and fixed assets.

Liabilities and Owners' Equity

Now let's consider the claims against those assets, beginning with a category called current liabilities. *Current liabilities* represent the claims of creditors and others that typically must be paid within a year; they include short-term IOUs, accrued salaries, accrued income taxes, and accounts payable. This year's repayment obligation on a long-term loan is also listed under current liabilities.

Subtracting current liabilities from current assets gives you the company's net working capital. *Net working capital* is the amount of money the company has tied up in its current (short-term) operating activities. Just how much is adequate for the company depends on the industry and the company's plans. In the balance sheet shown in table A-1, Amalgamated has $868,000 in net working capital.

Long-term liabilities are typically bonds and mortgages—debts that the company is contractually obliged to repay, with respect to both interest and principal.

According to the aforementioned accounting equation, total assets must equal total liabilities plus owners' equity. Thus, subtracting total liabilities from total assets, the balance sheet arrives at a figure for the owners' equity. Owners' equity comprises *retained earnings* (net profits that accumulate on a company's balance sheet after any

[handwritten margin note: Current assets - Current liabilities = net working capital.]

dividends are paid) and contributed capital (capital received in exchange for shares)

Historical Values

The values represented in many balance-sheet categories may not correspond to their actual market values. Except for items such as cash, accounts receivable, and accounts payable, the measurement of each classification will rarely be equal to the actual current value or cash value shown. This is because accountants must record most items at their historic cost. If, for example, XYZ's balance sheet indicated land worth $700,000, that figure would represent what XYZ paid for the land way back when. If the land was purchased in downtown San Francisco in 1960, you can bet that it is now worth immensely more than the value stated on the balance sheet.

So why do accountants use historic instead of market values? The short answer is that it represents the lesser of two evils. If market values were mandated, then every public company would be required to get a professional appraisal of every one of its properties, warehouse inventories, and so forth—and would have to do so every year. And how many people would trust those appraisals? So we're stuck with historic values on the balance sheet.

Managerial Issues

Although the balance sheet is prepared by accountants, it represents a number of important issues for managers.

WORKING CAPITAL. Business owners give substantial attention to the level of working capital, which naturally expands and contracts with sales activities. Too little working capital can put a company in a bad position: The company may be unable to pay its bills or to take advantage of profitable opportunities. Too much working capital, on the other hand, reduces profitability, because that capital has a carrying cost; it must be financed in some way, usually through interest-bearing loans.

Inventory is one component of working capital—unless yours is a service business that has no inventory. Like working capital in general, inventory must be balanced between too much and too little. Having lots of inventory on hand allows a company to fill customer orders without delay and provides a buffer against potential production stoppages and strikes. The flip side of plentiful inventory is the cost of financing and the risk of deterioration in the market value of the inventory itself. Every excess widget in the stockroom adds to the company's financing costs, and that reduces profits. And every item that sits on the shelf may become obsolete or less salable as time goes by—again, with a negative impact on profitability.

The personal computer business provides a clear example of how excess inventory can wreck the bottom line. Some analysts estimate that the value of finished-goods inventory melts away at a rate of approximately 2 percent *per day* because of technical obsolescence in this fast-moving industry.

FINANCIAL LEVERAGE. You have probably heard someone say, "It's a highly leveraged situation." Do you know what "leveraged" means in the financial sense? *Financial leverage* refers to the use of borrowed money in acquiring an asset. We say that a company is highly leveraged when the percentage of debt on its balance sheet is high relative to the capital invested by the owners. For example, suppose that you paid $400,000 for an asset, using $100,000 of your own money and $300,000 in borrowed funds. For simplicity, we'll ignore loan payments, taxes, and any cash flow you might get from the investment. Four years go by, and your asset has appreciated to $500,000. You decide to sell. After paying off the $300,000 loan, you end up with $200,000 in your pocket (your original $100,000 plus a $100,000 profit). That's a gain of 100 percent on your personal capital, even though the asset increased in value by only 25 percent. Financial leverage made this possible. In contrast, if you had financed the purchase entirely with your own funds ($400,000), then you would have ended up with only a 25 percent gain.

Financial leverage creates an opportunity for a company to gain a higher return on the capital invested by its owners. In the United

States and most other countries, tax policy makes financial leverage even more attractive by allowing businesses to deduct the interest paid on loans. But leverage can cut both ways. If the value of an asset drops (or fails to produce the anticipated level of revenue), then leverage works against its owner. Consider what would have happened in our example if the asset's value had dropped by $100,000, that is, to $300,000. The owner would have lost the entire $100,000 investment after repaying the initial loan of $300,000.

FINANCIAL STRUCTURE OF THE FIRM. The negative potential of financial leverage is what keeps CEOs from maximizing their debt financing. Instead, they seek a financial structure that creates a realistic balance between debt and equity on the balance sheet. Although leverage enhances a company's potential profitability as long as things go right, managers know that every dollar of debt increases the riskiness of the business—both because of the danger just cited and because high debt results in high interest payments, which must be paid in good times and bad. Many companies have failed when business reversals or recessions reduced their ability to make timely payments on their loans.

When creditors and investors examine corporate balance sheets, they look carefully at the debt-to-equity ratio. They factor the riskiness of the balance sheet into the interest they charge on loans and the return they demand from a company's bonds. Thus, a highly leveraged company may have to pay 14 percent on borrowed funds instead of the 10 to 12 percent paid by a less leveraged competitor. Investors also demand a higher rate of return for their stock investments in highly leveraged companies. They will not accept high risks without an expectation of commensurately large returns.

The Income Statement — *specified*

The income statement indicates the results of operations over a specified period. Those last two words are important. Unlike the balance sheet, which is a snapshot of the enterprise's position at a point in time, the *income statement* indicates cumulative business results within a defined time frame. It tells you whether the company is making a profit—that is, whether it has positive or negative net income (net earnings). This is why the income statement is often referred to as the *profit-and-loss statement,* or P&L. It shows a company's profitability at the end of a particular time—typically at the end of the month, the quarter, or the company's fiscal year. In addition, the income statement tells you how much money the company spent to make that profit—from which you can determine the company's *profit margin.*

As we did with the balance sheet, we can represent the contents of the income statement with a simple equation:

Revenues – Expenses = Net Income (or Net Loss)

An income statement starts with the company's *revenues:* the amount of money that results from selling products or services to customers. A company may have other revenues as well. In many cases, these are from investments or interest income from its cash holdings.

Various costs and expenses—from the costs of making and storing goods, to depreciation of plant and equipment, to interest expense and taxes—are then deducted from revenues. The bottom line—what's left over—is the *net income,* or net profit or net earnings, for the period of the statement.

Consider the meaning of various line items on the income statement for Amalgamated Hat Rack (table A-2). The *cost of goods sold* is what it cost Amalgamated to manufacture its hat racks. This figure includes the cost of raw materials, such as lumber, as well as the cost of turning them into finished goods, including direct labor costs. By deducting the cost of goods sold from sales revenue, we get a company's *gross profit*—the roughest estimation of the company's profitability.

The next major category of cost is *operating expenses*. Operating expenses include administrative employee salaries, rents, and sales and marketing costs, as well as other costs of business not directly attributed to the cost of manufacturing a product. The lumber for making hat racks would *not* be included here; the cost of the advertising and the salaries of Amalgamated administrative employees would be included.

TABLE A-2

Amalgamated Hat Rack Income Statement for the Fiscal Year Ending December 31, 2002

Retail Sales	$2,200,000
Corporate Sales	$1,000,000
Total Sales Revenue	$3,200,000
Less: Cost of Goods Sold	$1,600,000
Gross Profit	$1,600,000
Less: Operating Expenses	$800,000
Depreciation Expense	$42,500
Earnings before Interest and Taxes *GBIT*	$757,500
Less: Interest Expense	$110,000
Earnings before Income Tax	$647,500
Less: Income Tax	$300,000
Net Income	$347,500

Source: HMM Finance.

Depreciation is counted on the income statement as an expense, even though it involves no out-of-pocket payments. As described earlier, depreciation is a way of estimating the "consumption" of an asset, or the diminishing value of equipment, over time. A computer, for example, loses about one-third of its value each year. Thus, the company would not expense the full value of a computer in the first year of its purchase but rather would decrease its value as it is actually used over a span of three years. The idea behind depreciation is to recognize the diminished value of certain assets.

By subtracting operating expenses and depreciation from the gross profit, we get *operating earnings.* These earnings are often called earnings before interest and taxes, or EBIT.

We're now down to the last reductions in the path that revenues follow on their way to the bottom line. Interest expense is the interest

charged on loans a company has taken out. Income tax, tax levied by
the government on corporate income, is the final charge.

What revenues are left are referred to as net income, or earnings.
If net income is positive—as it is in the case of Amalgamated—we
have a profit, what the for-profit company lives for.

Making Sense of the Income Statement

As with the balance sheet, our analysis of a company's income statement is greatly aided when presented in a multiperiod format. This
allows us to spot trends and turnarounds. Most annual reports make
multiperiod data available, often going back five or more years.
Amalgamated's income statement in multiperiod form is depicted in
table A-3.

TABLE A-3

Amalgamated Hat Rack Multiperiod Income Statement

| | FOR THE PERIOD ENDING DECEMBER 31 | | | |
	2002	2001	2000	1999
Retail Sales	$2,200,000	$2,000,000	$1,720,000	$1,500,000
Corporate Sales	$1,000,000	$1,000,000	$1,100,000	$1,200,000
Total Sales Revenue	$3,200,000	$3,000,000	$2,820,000	$2,700,000
Less: Cost of Goods Sold	$1,600,000	$1,550,000	$1,400,000	$1,300,000
Gross Profit	$1,600,000	$1,450,000	$1,420,000	$1,400,000
Less: Operating Expenses	$800,000	$810,000	$812,000	$805,000
Depreciation Expense	$42,500	$44,500	$45,500	$42,500
Earnings before Interest and Taxes	$757,500	$595,500	$562,500	$552,500
Less: Interest Expense	$110,000	$110,000	$150,000	$150,000
Earnings before Income Tax	$647,500	$485,500	$412,500	$402,500
Less: Income Tax	$300,000	$194,200	$165,000	$161,000
Net Income	$347,500	$291,300	$247,500	$241,500

In this multiyear format, we observe that Amalgamated's annual retail sales have grown steadily, and its corporate sales have stagnated and even declined slightly. Operating expenses have stayed about the same, however, even as total sales have expanded. That's a good sign that management is holding the line on the cost of doing business. The company's interest expense has also declined, perhaps because it has paid off one of its loans. The bottom line, net income, has shown healthy growth.

The Cash Flow Statement

The *cash flow statement,* the last of the three essential financial statements, is the least used and understood. This statement details the reasons that the amount of cash (and cash equivalents) changed during the accounting period. More specifically, it reflects all changes in cash as affected by operating activities, investments, and financing activities. Like the bank statement you receive for your checking account, the cash flow statement tells how much cash was on hand at the beginning of the period and how much was on hand at the end. It then describes how the company acquired and spent cash in a particular period. The uses of cash are recorded as negative figures, and sources of cash are recorded as positive figures.

If you're a manager in a large corporation, changes in the company's cash flow typically don't have an impact on your day-to-day functioning. Nevertheless, it's a good idea to stay up-to-date with your company's cash flow projections, because they may come into play when you prepare your budget for the upcoming year. For example, if cash is tight, you will probably want to be conservative in your spending. Alternatively, if the company is flush with cash, you may have opportunities to make new investments. If you're a manager in a small company (or its owner), you're probably keenly aware of your cash flow situation and feel its impact almost every day.

The cash flow statement is useful because it indicates whether your company is turning accounts receivable into cash—and that ability is ultimately what will keep your company solvent. *Solvency* is the ability to pay bills as they come due.

As we did with the other statements, we can conceptualize the cash flow statement in terms of a simple equation:

Cash Flow from Profit + Other Sources of Cash – Uses of Cash = Change in Cash

Again using the Amalgamated Hat Rack example, we see that in its year 2002 cash flow statement, the company generated a positive cash flow of $377,900 (table A–4). The statement shows that cash

TABLE A-4

Amalgamated Hat Rack Cash Flow Statement, 2002

Net Income _Bottom Line_	$347,500
Operating Assets and Liabilities	
Accounts receivable	$(75,600)
Finished-goods inventory	$(125,000)
Prepaid expenses	$(37,000)
Accounts payable	$83,000
Accrued expenses	$25,000
Income tax payable	$(23,000)
Depreciation expense	$89,000
Total changes in operating assets and liabilities	$(63,600)
Cash flow from operations	$283,900
Investing Activities	
Sale of property, plant, and equipment	$267,000
Capital expenditures	$(175,000)
Cash flow from investing activities	$92,000
Financing Activities	
Short-term debt increase	$27,000
Long-term borrowing	$112,000
Capital stock	$50,000
Cash dividends to stockholders	$(187,000)
Cash flow from financing activities	$2,000
Increase in cash during year	$377,900

Source: HMM Finance.

flows from operations ($283,900) plus those from investing activities ($92,000) and from financing ($2,000) produced $377,900 in additional cash.

The cash flow statement doesn't measure the same thing as the income statement. If there is no cash transaction, then it cannot be reflected on a cash flow statement. Notice, however, that net income at the top of the cash flow statement is the same as the bottom line of the income statement; it's the company's profit. Through a series of adjustments, the cash flow statement translates this net income into a cash basis.

The statement's format reflects the three categories of activities that affect cash. Cash can be increased or decreased because of (1) operations, (2) the acquisition or sale of assets, that is, investments, or (3) changes in debt or stock or other financing activities. Let's consider each in turn, starting with operations:

- Accounts receivable and finished-goods inventory represent items the company has produced but for which it hasn't yet received payment. Prepaid expenses represent items the company has paid for but has not yet consumed. These items are all subtracted from cash flow.

- Accounts payable and accrued expenses represent items the company has already received or used but for which it hasn't yet paid. Consequently, these items add to cash flow.

Now consider investments. Investment activities include the following:

- Gains realized from the sale of plant, property, and equipment—in other words, gains realized from converting investments into cash

- Cash that the company uses to invest in financial instruments and plant, property, and equipment (the latter investments are often shown as capital expenditures)

The cash flow statement shows that Amalgamated has sold a building for $267,000 and has made capital expenditures of $175,000, for a net addition to cash flow of $92,000.

Cash Flow Versus Profit

Many people think of profits as cash flow. Don't make this mistake. For a particular period, profit may or may not contribute positively to cash flow. For example, if this year's profit derives from a huge sale made in November, the sale may be booked as revenues in the fiscal period, thus adding to profit. But if payment for that sale is not received until the next accounting period, it goes on the books as an account receivable, and that reduces cash flow.

Finally, we come to cash flow changes from financing activities. Amalgamated has raised money by increasing its short-term debt, by borrowing in the capital markets, and by issuing capital stock, thereby increasing its available cash flow. The dividends that Amalgamated pays, however ($187,000), must be paid out of cash flow and thus represent a decrease in cash flow.

There's a lot more to financial statements and their interpretation than we can provide in this short primer, but you now have a basis for learning more. The statements generated by your small start-up will be fairly simple in any case, and you can learn more as you work with your accountant or financial officer, and as your company grows.

Breakeven Analysis

A Useful Decision Tool

Whether they are planning their new business or making decisions about offering new products or services, entrepreneurs need to know the point at which they will begin making money. Breakeven analysis is a handy tool for this purpose. *Breakeven analysis* can tell you how much (or how much more) you need to sell in order to pay for a fixed investment—in other words, at what point you will break even. With that information in hand, you can look at market demand and competitors' market shares to determine whether it's realistic to expect to sell that much. Breakeven analysis can also help you think through the impact of changing price and volume relationships.

More specifically, the breakeven calculation helps you determine the volume level at which the total after-tax contribution from a product line or an investment covers its total fixed costs. But before you can perform the calculation, you need to understand the components that go into it.

Making the Calculation

To calculate breakeven, you must first understand three accounting concepts: fixed costs, variable costs, and contribution margin.

- **Fixed costs.** These are costs that stay mostly the same, no matter how many units of a product or service are sold—costs such as insurance, management salaries, and rent or lease payments.

For example, the rent on the production facility will remain the same whether the company makes ten thousand or twenty thousand units, and so will the cost of insurance.

- **Variable costs.** Variable costs are those that change with the number of units produced and sold; examples include utilities, labor, and the costs of raw materials. The more units you make, the more you consume these items. Sales commissions are another variable cost.

- **Contribution margin.** This is the amount of money that every sold unit contributes to paying for fixed costs. It is defined as net unit revenue minus variable (or direct) costs per unit.

With these concepts understood, we can make the calculation. We are looking for the solution to this straightforward equation:

Breakeven Volume = Fixed Costs / Unit Contribution Margin

Here's how we do it. First, find the unit contribution margin by subtracting the variable costs per unit from the net revenue per unit. Then divide total fixed costs, or the amount of the investment, by the unit contribution margin. The quotient is the breakeven volume, that is, the number of units that must be sold in order for all fixed costs to be covered.

Let's consider a hypothetical situation. Amalgamated Hat Rack, Inc., is planning to sell its new plastic wall-mounted hat rack for $75 per unit. The company's variable cost per unit is $22. It will spend $100,000 (a fixed cost) for the plastic extruder that will make these hat racks. Thus

$75 (Price per Unit) – $22 (Variable Cost per Unit) = $53 (Unit Contribution Margin)

Therefore

$100,000 (Total Investment Required) / $53 (Unit Contribution Margin) = 1,887 Units

The preceding calculations indicate that Amalgamated must sell 1,887 hat racks to break even on its $100,000 investment.

At this point, Amalgamated must decide whether the breakeven volume is achievable: Is it realistic to expect to sell 1,887 additional hat racks, and if so, how quickly?

A Breakeven Complication

Our hat rack breakeven analysis represents a simple case. It assumes that costs are distinctly fixed or variable, that costs and unit contributions will not change as a function of volume (i.e., that the sale price of the item under consideration will not change at different levels of output; rent will stay the same whether one thousand or ten thousand units are produced and sold).

These assumptions may not hold in your more complicated world. Rent may be fixed up to a certain level of production and then increase by 50 percent as you rent a secondary facility to handle expanded output. Labor costs may in reality be a hybrid of fixed and variable. And as you push more of your product into the market, you may find it necessary to offer price discounts, and that will reduce contribution per unit. You must adjust the breakeven calculation to accommodate these untidy realities.

Operating Leverage

Your goal as an entrepreneur, of course, is not to break even but to make a profit. After you've covered all your fixed costs with the contributions of many unit sales, every subsequent sale contributes directly to profits. As we observed earlier,

Unit Net Revenue − Unit Variable Cost = Contribution to Profit

You can see at a glance that the lower the unit variable cost, the greater the contribution to profits will be. In the pharmaceutical business, for example, the unit cost of cranking out and packaging a bottle of a new wonder drug may be less than a dollar. Yet if the company can sell each bottle for $100, a whopping sum of $99 contributes to corporate profits after sales have gotten beyond the breakeven point! The trouble is that the pharmaceutical company may have invested $400 million up front in fixed product development costs just to get the first bottle out the door. It will have to sell many bottles of the new medication just to break even. But when it does, profits can be extraordinary.

The relationship between fixed and variable costs is often described in terms of *operating leverage*. Companies whose fixed costs are high relative to their variable costs are said to have high operating leverage. The pharmaceutical business, for example, generally operates with high operating leverage. So too does the software industry: The greater percentage of its costs are fixed product development outlays; the variable cost of the CDs on which programs are distributed represents only pennies.

Now consider the opposite: low operating leverage. Here, fixed costs are low relative to the total cost of producing each unit of output. A consulting business is a good example of one that functions with low operating leverage. The firm has a minimal investment in equipment and fixed expenses. The bulk of its costs are the fees it pays its consultants, which vary depending on the actual hours they bill to clients.

Operating leverage is a great thing after a company passes its breakeven point, but it can cause substantial losses if breakeven is never achieved. In other words, it's risky. This is why managers give much thought to finding the right balance between fixed and variable costs.

Valuation Concepts

What Is a Business Really Worth?

What is your business worth? This is a question that most entrepreneurs must eventually answer because they are either buying an existing business or selling one of their own. And answering it correctly is extremely important. If you pay too much for a business, your rate of return will be disappointing. Similarly, if you underestimate the value of an entity you are selling, you will shortchange yourself without knowing it.

Valuing an ongoing business—large or small—is neither easy nor exact. In most cases it is the domain of experts. But the subject is too important to leave to experts. As an entrepreneur you should be familiar with the various valuation approaches used by experts, including their strengths and their weaknesses. You'll find those approaches discussed here.[1]

But before we get started, consider these cautions. The true value of a business is never knowable with certainty. You may seek it, but you can never be sure that you have found the true value of the business. This lack of certainty is the result of two problems. First, alternative valuation methods consistently fail to produce the same outcome, even when meticulously calculated. Second, the product of valuation methods is only as good as the data and the estimates we bring to them, and these are often incomplete, unreliable, or based on projections. For example, one method depends heavily on estimates of future cash flows. In the very best cases, those estimates will only be close. In the worst cases, they will be far from the mark.

Another consideration is that a company is worth different amounts to different parties. Different prospective buyers are likely to assign different values to the same set of assets. For example, if you were a book collector who already owned first editions of every Hemingway novel except *For Whom the Bell Tolls,* then that book would be much more valuable to you than it would be to another collector who owned only one or two first-edition Hemingways. The reason? For you, the acquisition would complete a set, whose value is greater than the sum of the individual volumes considered separately. Businesses look on acquisitions with a similar perspective. The acquisition of a small, high-tech company, for example, might provide the acquirer with the technology it needs to leverage its other operations. This explains, in part, why many firms are purchased for more than the market value of their existing shares.

It is also important to keep in mind that valuation is the province of specialists. Small and closely held businesses typically turn to professional appraisers when their value must be established for the purpose of a sale, to determine the value of its shares when an employee stock ownership plan is used, or for some other purpose. When large, public firms or their business units are the subjects of a valuation, executives generally turn to a variety of full-service accounting, investment banking, or consulting firms. Many of these vendors have departments devoted entirely to mergers and acquisitions, in which valuation issues are a central focus. A well-rounded entrepreneur cannot be an expert in these matters, but you should understand the nature of various valuation methods along with their strengths and weaknesses.

Valuation problems often arise in the context of closely held businesses—that is, businesses with only a few owners—or in the sale of an operating unit of a public company. In neither case are there publicly traded ownership shares. Public markets for ownership, such as NASDAQ or the New York Stock Exchange, make value more transparent. Everyday buying and selling in these markets establishes a company's per-share price. And that price, multiplied by the number of outstanding shares, often provides a basis for a fair approximation of company's value at a point in time. But this basis is not available in the absence of public trading.

Asset–Based Valuations

One way to value an enterprise is to determine the value of its assets. There are four approaches to asset-based valuations: equity book value, adjusted book value, liquidation value, and replacement value.

Equity Book Value

Equity book value is the simplest valuation approach and uses the balance sheet as its primary source of information. Here's the formula:

Equity Book Value = Total Assets − Total Liabilities

To test this formula, consider the balance sheet of Amalgamated Hat Rack Company, which we encountered in appendix A. Table A-1 showed total assets of $3,635,000 and total liabilities of $1,750,000. The difference—the equity book value—is $1,885,000. Notice that this is the same as total owners' equity. In other words, if you reduce the balance sheet (or book) value of the business's assets by the amount of its debts and other financial obligations, you have its equity value.

This equity-book-value approach is easy and quick. And it is common for executives in a particular industry to roughly calculate their company's value in the context of equity book value. For example, one owner might contend that his company is worth at least book value in a sale because that was the amount that he invested in the business. But equity book value is not a reliable guide for businesses in many industries. The reason is that assets are placed on the balance sheet at their historical costs, which may not be their value today. The value of balance-sheet assets may be unrealistic for other reasons as well. Consider Amalgamated's assets:

- Accounts receivable could be suspect if many accounts are uncollectible.

- Inventory reflects historic cost, but inventory may be worthless or less valuable than its stated balance-sheet value (or "book" value) because of spoilage or obsolescence. Or some inventory may be undervalued.

- Property, plant, and equipment depreciation should also be closely examined—particularly land. If Amalgamated's property was put on the books in 1975—and if it happens to be in the heart of San Francisco—then its real market value may be ten or twenty times the 1975 figure.

The preceding are only a few examples that illustrate why book value is not always true market value.

Adjusted Book Value

The weaknesses of the quick-and-dirty equity-book-value approach have led some to adopt *adjusted book value,* which attempts to restate the value of balance-sheet assets to realistic market levels. Consider the influence of adjusted book value in a leverage buyout of a major retail store chain in the 1990s. At the time of the analysis, the store chain had an equity book value of $1.3 billion. After its inventory and property assets were adjusted to their appraised values, however, the enterprise's value leaped to $2.2 billion—an increase of 69 percent.

When asset values are adjusted, it is essential to determine the real value of any listed intangibles, such as goodwill and patents. In most cases, goodwill is an accounting fiction created when one company buys another at a premium to book value—that is, at a price higher than book value. The premium must be put on the balance sheet as goodwill. But to a potential buyer, the intangible asset may have no value.

Liquidation Value

Liquidation value is similar to adjusted book value. It attempts to restate balance-sheet values in terms of the net cash that would be realized if assets were disposed of in a quick sale and all liabilities of the company were paid off or otherwise settled. This approach recognizes that many assets, especially inventory and fixed assets, usually do not fetch as much as they would if the sale were made more deliberately.

Replacement Value

Some people use *replacement value* to obtain a rough estimate of value. This method simply estimates the cost of reproducing the business's assets. Of course, a buyer may not want to replicate all the assets included in the sale price of a company. In this case, the replacement value represents more than the value that the buyer would place on the company.

The various asset-based valuation approaches described here generally share some strengths and weakness. On the positive side, asset-based methods are easy and inexpensive to calculate. They are also easy to understand. On the negative side, both equity book value and liquidation value fail to reflect the actual market value of assets. And all these approaches fail to recognize the intangible value of an ongoing enterprise, which derives much of its wealth-generating power from human knowledge, skill, and reputation.

Earnings-Based Valuation

Another approach to valuing a company is to capitalize its earnings. This involves multiplying one or another income statement earnings figure (e.g., earnings before income tax) by some figure. Some earnings-based methods, however, are more sophisticated.

Earnings Multiple

For a publicly traded company, the current share price multiplied by the number of outstanding shares indicates the market value of the company's equity. Add to this the value of the company's debt, and you have the total value of the enterprise. In other words, the total value of the company is the equity of the owners *plus* any outstanding debt. Why add the debt? Consider your own home. When you go to sell your house, you don't set the price at the level of your equity in the property. Rather, its value is the total of the outstanding debt and your equity interest. Similarly, the value of a company is shareholders' equity plus the liabilities. This is often referred to as the *enterprise value.*

For a public company whose shares are priced by the market every business day, pricing the equity is straightforward. But what about a closely held corporation, whose share price is generally unknown because such a firm does not trade in a public market? We can reach a value estimate by using the known *price-earnings multiple* (often called the *P/E ratio*) of similar enterprises that are publicly traded. The price-earnings approach to share value begins with this formula:

Share Price = Current Earnings × Multiple

We calculate the multiple from comparable publicly traded companies as follows:

Multiple = Share Price / Current Earnings

Thus, if XYZ Corporation's shares are trading at $50 per share and its current earnings are $5 per share, then the multiple is 10. In stock market parlance, we'd say that XYZ is trading at ten times earnings.

We can use this multiple approach to pricing the equity of a nonpublic corporation if we can find one or more similar enterprises with known price-earnings multiples. This is a challenge, because no two enterprises are exactly alike. The uniqueness of every business is the reason valuation experts recognize their work as part science and part art.

To examine this method further, let's return to our sample firm. Because Amalgamated Hat Rack is a closely held firm, we have no readily available benchmark for valuing its shares. But let's suppose that we were successful in identifying a publicly traded company (or, even better, several companies) similar to Amalgamated in most respects—both as to industry and as to size. We'll call one of these firms Acme Corporation. And let's suppose that Acme's P/E ratio is 8. Let's also suppose that our crack researchers have discovered that another company, this one private and in the same industry as Amalgamated, was recently acquired at roughly the same multiple: 8. This gives us confidence that our multiple of 8 is in the ballpark.

With this information, let's revisit Amalgamated's income statement presented in appendix A (table A-2), where we find that its net income (earnings) is $347,500. Plugging the relevant numbers in to the following formula, we estimate Amalgamated's value:

Earnings × Appropriate Multiple = Equity Value
$347,500 × 8 = $2,780,000

Remember that this is the value of the company's equity. To find the total enterprise value of Amalgamated, we must add the total of its interest-bearing liabilities. Table A-1 in appendix A shows that the company's interest-bearing liabilities (short-term and long-term debt) for 2002 are $1,175,000. Thus, the value of the entire enterprise is as follows:

Enterprise Value = Equity Value + Value of Interest-Bearing Debt
$3,955,000 = $2,780,000 + $1,175,000

The effectiveness of the multiple approach to valuation depends in part on the reliability of the earnings figure. The most recent earnings might, for example, be unnaturally depressed by a one-time write-off of obsolete inventory or pumped up by the sale of a subsidiary company. For this reason, it is essential that you factor out random and nonrecurring items. Similarly, you should review expenses to determine that they are normal—neither extraordinarily high nor extraordinarily low. For example, inordinately low maintenance charges over a period of time would pump up near-term earnings but would result in extraordinary expenses in the future for deferred maintenance. Similarly, nonrecurring, windfall sales can also distort the earnings picture.

In small, closely held companies, you need to pay particular attention to the salaries of the owner-managers and the members of their families. If these salaries have been unreasonably high or low, an adjustment of earnings is required. You should also assess the depreciation rates to determine their validity and, if necessary, to make appropriate adjustments to reported earnings.

EBIT Multiple

The reliability of the multiple approach to valuation just described depends on the comparability of the firm or firms used as proxies for the target company. In the Amalgamated example, we relied heavily on the observed earnings multiple of Acme Corporation, a publicly traded company whose business is similar to Amalgamated's. Unfortunately, these two companies could produce equal operating results and yet indicate much different bottom-line profits to their shareholders.

How is this possible? The answer is twofold: The two companies show different bottom lines because of the manner in which they are financed and because of taxes. If a company is heavily financed with debt, its interest expenses will be large, and those expenses will reduce the total dollars available to the owners at the bottom line. Similarly, one company's tax bill might be much higher than the other's for some reason that has little to do with its future wealth-producing capabilities. And taxes reduce bottom-line earnings.

Consider the hypothetical scenario in table C-1. Notice that the two companies produce the same earnings before interest and taxes (EBIT). But because Acme uses more debt and less equity in financing its assets, its interest expense is much higher ($350,000 versus $110,000). This dramatically reduces its earnings before income

TABLE C-1

Hypothetical Income Statements of Amalgamated Hat Rack and Acme Corporation

	Amalgamated	Acme
Earnings before Interest and Taxes	$757,500	$757,500
Less: Interest Expense	$110,000	$350,000
Earnings before Income Tax	$647,500	$407,500
Less: Income Tax	$300,000	$187,000
Net Income	$347,500	$220,500

taxes compared with that of Amalgamated. Even though each pays an equal percentage in income taxes, Acme ends up with substantially lower bottom-line earnings.

This earnings variation between two otherwise comparable enterprises would produce different equity values. The problem can be circumvented by using EBIT instead of bottom-line earnings in the valuation process. Some practitioners go one step further and use the EBITDA multiple (EBIT plus depreciation and amortization). Depreciation and amortization are noncash charges against bottom-line earnings—accounting allocations that tend to create differences between otherwise similar firms. By using EBITDA in the valuation equation, you avoid this potential distortion.

Discounted Cash Flow Method

One big problem with the earnings-based methods just described is that they are based on historical performance—what happened last year. But past performance is no assurance of future results. If you were making an offer to buy a local small business, chances are that you'd base your offer on its ability to produce profits in the years *ahead*. Similarly, if your company were hatching plans to acquire Amalgamated Hat Rack, it would be less interested in what Amalgamated earned in the past than in what it is likely to earn in the future under new management.

We can direct our earnings-based valuation toward the future by using a more sophisticated valuation method: *discounted cash flow* (DCF). The DCF valuation method is based on time-value-of-money concepts. DCF determines value by calculating the present value of a business's future cash flows, including its terminal value. Because those cash flows are available to both equity holders and debt holders, DCF can reflect the value of the enterprise as a whole or can be confined to the cash flows left available to shareholders.

Time value concepts are not covered in this book, but are explained in all textbooks on finance and in *Harvard Business Essentials: Finance for Managers* (Harvard Business School Press, 2003).

The DCF method has numerous strengths:

- It recognizes the time value of future cash flows.

- It is future oriented and estimates future cash flows in terms of what the new owner could achieve.

- It accounts for the buyer's cost of capital.

- It does not depend on comparisons with similar companies—comparisons that are bound to be different in various dimensions (e.g., earnings-based multiples).

- It is based on real cash flows instead of accounting values.

The weakness of the DCF method is that it assumes that future cash flows, including the terminal value, can be estimated with reasonable accuracy. This is rarely the case for cash flow estimates made far into the future.

Clearly, the information given here will not make you a competent valuation practitioner, but with a little reflection it should put you in a better position to deal with those practitioners in negotiating the sale of your own company or the purchase of another.

Summing Up

The important but difficult subject of business valuation can be summarized in three types of approaches:

- **Asset-based.** This valuation approach includes the use of equity book value, adjusted book value, liquidation value, or replacement value. In general, these methods are easy to calculate and understand but have notable weaknesses. Except for replacement and adjusted book methods, they fail to reflect the actual market values of assets; they also fail to recognize the intangible value of an ongoing enterprise, which derives much of its wealth-generating power from human knowledge, skill, and reputation.

- **Earnings–based.** This valuation approach includes the price-earnings method, the EBIT method, and the EBITDA method. The earnings-based approach is generally superior to asset-based methods, but it depends on the availability of comparable businesses whose P/E multiples are known.

- **Cash–flow–based.** This method is based on the concepts of the time value of money. The DCF method has many advantages, the most important being its future-looking orientation. The method estimates future cash flows in terms of what a new owner could achieve. It also recognizes the buyer's cost of capital. The major weakness of the method is the difficulty inherent in producing reliable estimates of future cash flows.

In the end, these approaches to valuation are bound to produce different outcomes. Even the same method applied by two experienced professionals can produce different results. For this reason, most appraisers use more than one method in approximating the true value of an asset or a business.

Online Help When You Need It

Entrepreneurs can draw from many sources of information and advice. Some of the best are bankers, local business schools, and other businesspeople in your own community. You can also find plenty of help via the Internet. "Plenty" is an understatement. A person could spend days exploring the many sites and links dedicated to entrepreneurs and small business owners. Here is a short list and description of the most useful sites:

www.bplan.com

This site has lots of advice, sample business plans, and a number of helpful "calculators" that you can use to estimate start-up cash requirements, cash flow, and breakeven. There is also a useful database of articles on a wide range of topics, such as the pros and cons of buying a franchise, buying an underperforming business, business valuation, finding investment angels, and so forth. These articles are not very deep, but they will get you thinking in the right direction.

www.businessfinance.com

This site has a number of free, downloadable booklets in PDF format that will help you build your credit profile, present a funding request, and do business with angel and venture investors.

www.sba.gov

This is the mother of all sites for the small business, with information and advice on everything from the basics of business start-up to business planning, finance, marketing, taxes, legal issues, and more. It's all courtesy of the U.S. Small Business Administration. There's even a self-administered diagnostic test you can take to determine whether you have the makings of an entrepreneur. Perhaps the most valuable items on the site are as follows:

- **Online courses covering dozens of topics.** These are fairly thorough. Most have audio clips and self-tests, and some have interactive worksheets you can use to create a cash flow statement, write a business plan, and so forth. Master the material in these courses and you could become a small-business consultant.

- **Information on SBA loans and who qualifies for them.** The SBA offers numerous financing programs to assist small businesses. Women, minorities, the disabled, veterans of the U.S. armed forces, and low-income citizens may qualify for special financing options.

www.entrepreneur.com

This is the site for *Entrepreneur Magazine*. It features many how-to guides on various aspects of small-business ownership and operations, as well as links to expert advice on dozens of subjects. Check the archive of past articles that may pertain to your business. The January edition always lists the top ten U.S. franchise opportunities, with supporting data on investment and fee requirements, training, and owner qualification.

www.score.org

SCORE ("Counselors to America's Small Business") is a nonprofit organization based in Washington, D.C., that provides entrepreneurs with free face-to-face and e-mail business counseling. Counseling and low-cost workshops are offered at 389 chapter offices across the United States by SCORE's ten thousand five hundred retired and volunteer businesspeople. For the office nearest you, check the site's handy locator.

Need advice in a hurry? The SCORE site features many "60 second guides" on the usual problems, such as how to do a better job of collecting accounts receivable, creating a market niche, and so on.

You can also submit a specific question online and expect one of SCORE's one thousand two hundred online counselors to answer via e-mail within twenty-four hours.

www.businesspartners.com

Looking for equity capital? Business Partners, according to the site's home page, is a global, Internet-based service that connects entrepreneurs, early-stage companies, and corporate investors. Links on this site will take you to many informative sites, including those that deal with locating angel investors and seeing your business plan from the investor's perspective.

www.antiventurecapital.com/vc9ad1.html

Think you have a chance of getting venture funding? Before you get your hopes up, check out this anti-VC site. It will sober you up—and perhaps save you many wasted months of searching and sending out business plans that will never be read.

www.hoovers.com/ global/ipoc/index.xhtml

This site tells you which companies are poised to go public (are on deck) at the moment. It provides a thumbnail sketch of these companies, their revenues, their number of employees, the amount of money they are seeking, and so forth. It also allows you to look through a list of companies that have recently gone public; handy price charts reveal at a glance whether shareholders have won or lost money since their issue dates.

Rule 144

Selling Restricted and Control Securities

The trading of common stock acquired before an IPO is "restricted" by the U.S. Securities and Exchange Commission. A number of rules govern how that restriction can be lifted. Here is the SEC's own description of its key rule governing restricted shares.

When you acquire restricted securities or hold control securities, you must find an exemption from the SEC's registration requirements to sell them in the marketplace. Rule 144 allows public resale of restricted and control securities if a number of conditions are met. This overview tells you what you need to know about selling your restricted or control securities. It also describes how to have a restrictive legend removed.

What Are Restricted and Control Securities?

Restricted securities are securities acquired in unregistered, private sales from the issuer or from an affiliate of the issuer. Investors typically receive restricted securities through private placement offerings, Regulation D offerings, employee stock benefit plans, as compensation for professional services, or in exchange for providing "seed money" or start-up capital to the company. Rule 144(a)(3) identifies what sales produce restricted securities.

Control securities are those held by an affiliate of the issuing company. An affiliate is a person, such as a director or large shareholder, in a relationship of control with the issuer. Control means the power to direct the management and policies of the company in question, whether through the ownership of voting securities, by contract, or otherwise. If you buy securities from a controlling person or "affiliate," you take restricted securities, even if they were not restricted in the affiliate's hands.

If you acquire restricted securities, you almost always will receive a certificate stamped with a "restricted" legend. The legend indicates that the securities may not be resold in the marketplace unless they are registered with the SEC or are exempt from the registration requirements. The certificates of control securities are usually not stamped with a legend.

What Are the Conditions of Rule 144?

If you want to sell your restricted or control securities to the public, you can follow the conditions set forth in Rule 144. The rule is not the exclusive means for selling restricted or control securities, but provides a "safe harbor" exemption to sellers. The rule's five conditions are summarized below:

1. **Holding Period.** Before you may sell restricted securities in the marketplace, you must hold them for at least one year. The one-year holding period begins when the securities were bought and fully paid for. The holding period only applies to restricted securities. Because securities acquired in the public market are not restricted, there is no holding period for an affiliate who purchases securities of the issuer in the marketplace. But an affiliate's resale is subject to the other conditions of the rule.

   Additional securities purchased from the issuer do not affect the holding period of previously purchased securities of the same class. If you purchased restricted securities from another non-affiliate, you can tack on that non-affiliate's holding period to your holding period. For gifts made by an affiliate, the holding period begins when the affiliate acquired the securities and not on the date of the gift. In the case of a stock option, such as one an employee receives, the holding period always begins as of the date the option is exercised and not the date it is granted.

2. **Adequate Current Information.** There must be adequate current information about the issuer of the securities before the sale can be made. This generally means the issuer has complied with the periodic reporting requirements of the Securities Exchange Act of 1934.

3. **Trading Volume Formula.** After the one-year holding period, the number of shares you may sell during any three-month period can't exceed the greater of 1% of the outstanding shares of the same class being sold, or if the class is listed on a stock exchange or quoted on NASDAQ, the greater of 1% or the average reported weekly trading volume during the four weeks preceding the filing of a notice of the sale on Form 144. Over-the-counter stocks, including those quoted on the OTC Bulletin Board and the Pink Sheets, can only be sold using the 1% measurement.

4. **Ordinary Brokerage Transactions.** The sales must be handled in all respects as routine trading transactions, and brokers may not receive more than a normal commission. Neither the seller nor the broker can solicit orders to buy the securities.

5. **Filing Notice With the SEC.** At the time you place your order, you must file a notice with the SEC on Form 144 if the sale involves more than 500 shares or the aggregate dollar amount is greater than $10,000 in any three-month period. The sale must take place within three months of filing the Form and, if the securities have not been sold, you must file an amended notice.

If you are not an affiliate of the issuer and have held restricted securities for two years, you can sell them without regard to the above conditions.

Can the Securities Be Sold Publicly If the Conditions of Rule 144 Have Been Met?

Even if you have met the conditions of Rule 144, you can't sell your restricted securities to the public until you've gotten the legend removed from the certificate. Only a transfer agent can remove a restrictive legend. But the transfer agent won't remove the legend unless you've obtained the consent of the issuer—usually in the form of an opinion letter from the issuer's counsel—that the restricted legend can be removed. Unless this happens, the transfer agent doesn't have the authority to remove the legend and execute the trade in the marketplace.

To begin the process, an investor should contact the company that issued the securities, or the transfer agent of the company's securities, to ask about the procedures for removing a legend. Since removing the legend can be a complicated process, if you're considering buying or selling a restricted security, it would be wise for you to consult an attorney who specializes in securities law.

What If a Dispute Arises Over Whether I Can Remove the Legend?

If a dispute arises about whether a restricted legend can be removed, the SEC will not intervene. The removal of a legend is a matter solely in the discretion of the issuer of the securities. State law, not federal law, covers disputes about the removal of legends. Thus, the SEC will not take action in any decision or dispute about removing a restrictive legend.

Source: U.S. Securities and Exchange Commission
http://www.sec.gov/investor/pubs/rule144.htm

Notes

Introduction

1. William D. Bygrave, ed., *The Portable MBA in Entrepreneurship,* 2nd edition (New York: John Wiley & Sons, 1997), 2.

2. William E. Wetzel Jr., "Venture Capital," in *The Portable MBA in Entrepreneurship*, 2nd edition, ed. William D. Bygrave (New York: John Wiley & Sons, 1997), 185.

Chapter 1

1. William D. Bygrave, ed., *The Portable MBA in Entrepreneurship,* 2nd edition (New York: John Wiley & Sons, 1997).

2. Walter Kuemmerle, "A Test for the Fainthearted," *Harvard Business Review,* May 2002, 122–127.

3. Ibid., 122.

4. Ibid., 125.

5. Dan Bricklin, "Natural-Born Entrepreneur," *Harvard Business Review,* September 2001, 53-59.

Chapter 2

1. Jeffry A. Timmons, *New Venture Creation*, 6th edition (Burr Ridge, Illinois: McGraw Hill-Irwin, 2004), 119–120.

2. Jeffry A. Timmons, "Opportunity Recognition," in *The Portable MBA in Entrepreneurship*, 2nd edition, ed. William D. Bygrave (New York: John Wiley & Sons, 1997).

3. David Bovet and Joseph Martha, *Value Nets* (New York: John Wiley & Sons, 2000), 40.

Chapter 4

1. Richard G. Hamermesh and Paul W. Marshall, "Note on Business Model Analysis for the Entrepreneur," Class Note 9-802-048, Harvard Business School Publishing, Boston, 22 January 2002, 1.

2. Joan Magretta, "Why Business Models Matter," *Harvard Business Review*, May 2002, 86–92.

3. David Bunnell, (with Richard Luecke) *The eBay Phenomenon* (New York: John Wiley & Sons, 2000), 77.

4. Bruce Henderson, "The Origin of Strategy," *Harvard Business Review*, November–December 1989.

5. Michael E. Porter, "What Is Strategy?" *Harvard Business Review*, November–December 1996: 61–78.

6. Ibid.

7. Ibid., 12–13.

8. Ibid., 12.

9. Professor Alfred E. Osborne, memo to writer, 21 March 2004.

Chapter 5

1. William A. Sahlman, "How to Write a Great Business Plan," *Harvard Business Review*, July–August 1997, 100–101.

2. The Harvard Business Essentials Web site contains a free, downloadable computer spreadsheet template you can use to develop a pro forma balance sheet, an income statement, and a cash flow statement for your business plan. It will also produce several charts that readers of your plan will find useful. This piece of software comes with complete instructions. To access it, go to www.elearning.hbsp.org/businesstools.

3. William Strunk Jr. and E. B. White, *The Elements of Style,* 3rd edition (New York: Macmillan Publishing Company, 1979), 23.

Chapter 6

1. Amar Bhidé, "Bootstrap Finance: The Art of Start-ups," in *The Entrepreneurial Venture*, 2nd edition, eds. William A. Sahlman, Howard Stevenson, Michael Roberts, and Amar Bhidé (Boston: Harvard Business School Press, 1999), 224.

2. Ibid.

3. For the complete story of eBay's evolution, see David Bunnell (with Richard Luecke), *The eBay Phenomenon* (New York: John Wiley & Sons, 2000), 17–30. All financial information about the company described here is from eBay's 2001 10-K form.

Chapter 7

1. William E. Wetzel Jr., "Venture Capital," in *The Portable MBA in Entrepreneurship,* 2nd edition, ed. William D. Bygrave (New York: John Wiley & Sons, 1997), 185.

2. Ibid., 186.

3. Mark Van Osnabrugge and Robert J. Robinson, *Angel Investing: Matching Startup Funds with Startup Companies—A Guide for Entrepreneurs, Individual Investors, and Venture Capitalists* (San Francisco: Jossey-Bass, 2000), 5.

4. "The Angel Investors Are Here" <http://www.angel-investing.org/angel-directory-3.html> (accessed 28 January 2004).

5. The European Business Angel Network, <www.eban.org> (accessed 26 January 2004).

6. For a full treatment of the technical and legal issues of venture capital deal making, see Constance Bagley and Craig Dauchy, "Venture Capital," in *The Entrepreneurial Venture*, 2nd edition, eds. William A. Sahlman, Howard H. Stevenson, Michael J. Roberts, and Amar Bhidé (Boston: Harvard Business School Press, 1999), 262–303.

Chapter 8

1. Stephen C. Blowers, Peter H. Griffith, and Thomas L. Milan, *The Ernst & Young Guide to the IPO Value Journey* (New York: John Wiley & Sons, 1999), 8.

Chapter 9

1. Amar Bhidé, "Building the Self-Sustaining Firm," Class Note 395–200, Harvard Business School Publishing, Boston, 1995.

2. Michael J. Roberts, "Managing Transitions in the Growing Enterprise," Class Note 393–107, Harvard Business School Publishing, Boston, 1993.

3. Ibid., 388.

4. Eric G. Flamholtz and Yvonne Randle, *Growing Pains: Transitioning from an Entrepreneurship to a Professionally Managed Firm*, revised edition (San Francisco: Jossey-Bass, 2000), 11.

5. Ibid., xvii.

Chapter 10

1. Michael L. Tushman and Charles A. O'Reilly III, *Winning Through Innovation* (Boston, MA: Harvard Business School Press, 1997), 33–34.

2. Ibid., 219.

Chapter 11

1. T. A. Soja and J. E. Reyes, *Investment Benchmarks: Venture Capital* (Needham, MA: Venture Economics, 1990), 191.

2. Tom Copeland, Tim Koller, and Jack Murrin, *Valuation: Measuring and Managing the Value of Companies*, 2nd edition (New York: John Wiley & Sons, 1994), 70.

Appendix C

1. This chapter contains material adapted from Michael J. Robert, "Valuation Techniques," Class Note 9-384-185, Harvard Business School Publishing, Boston, revised 18 August 1988.

Glossary

ACCOUNTS PAYABLE   A category of balance-sheet liabilities representing moneys owed by the company.

ACCOUNTS RECEIVABLE   A category of balance-sheet assets representing moneys owed to the company by customers and others.

ACID-TEST RATIO   The ratio of so-called quick assets (cash, marketable security, and accounts receivable) to current liabilities. Unlike the current ratio, inventory is left out of the calculation.

ADJUSTED BOOK VALUE   A refinement of the book value method of valuation that attempts to restate the value of certain assets on the balance sheet according to realistic market values.

ANGEL   See *Business angel*.

ASSETS   The balance-sheet items in which a company invests so that it can conduct business. Examples include cash and financial instruments, inventories of raw materials and finished goods, land, buildings, and equipment. Assets also include moneys owed to the company by customers and others—an asset category referred to as accounts receivable.

BALANCE SHEET   A financial statement that describes the assets owned by the business and shows how those assets are financed—with the funds of creditors (liabilities), the equity of the owners, or both. Also known as the statement of financial position.

BOND   A debt security usually issued with a fixed interest rate and a stated maturity date. The bond issuer has a contractual obligation to make periodic interest payments and to redeem the bond at its face value on maturity.

BOOK VALUE OF SHAREHOLDER EQUITY A balance-sheet valuation method that calculates value as total assets less total liabilities.

BOOTSTRAP FINANCING A form of start-up financing in which the founders rely on their own personal financial resources and those of friends, family, employees, and suppliers to launch the business.

BREAKEVEN ANALYSIS A form of analysis that helps determine how much (or how much more) a company needs to sell in order to pay for the fixed investment—in other words, at what point the company will break even on its cash flow.

BUSINESS ANGEL A high-net-worth individual, usually a successful businessperson or professional, who provides early-stage capital to a start-up business in the form of debt, ownership capital, or both.

BUSINESS MODEL A conceptual description of an enterprise's revenue sources, cost drivers, investment size, and success factors and how they work together.

BUSINESS PLAN A document that explains a business opportunity, identifies the market to be served, and provides details about how the entrepreneurial organization plans to pursue it. Ideally it describes the unique qualifications that the management team brings to the effort, defines the resources required for success, and provides a forecast of results over a reasonable time horizon.

CAPITAL MARKETS The financial markets in which long-term debt instruments and equity securities—including private placements—are issued and traded.

CASH FLOW STATEMENT A financial statement that details the reasons for changes in cash (and cash equivalents) during the accounting period. More specifically, it reflects all changes in cash as affected by operating activities, investments, and financing activities.

C CORPORATION In the United States, an entity chartered by the state and treated as a person under the law. The C corporation can have an infinite number of owners. Ownership is evidenced by shares of company stock. The entity is managed on behalf of shareholders—at least indirectly—by a board of directors.

COLLATERAL An asset pledged to the lender until such time as the loan is satisfied.

COMMERCIAL PAPER A short-term financing instrument used primarily by large, creditworthy corporations as an alternative to short-term bank borrowing. Most paper is sold at a discount to its face value and is redeemable at face value on maturity.

COMMON STOCK A security that represents a fractional ownership interest in the corporation that issued it.

COST OF GOODS SOLD On the income statement, what it costs a company to produce its goods and services. This figure includes raw materials, production, and direct labor costs.

CURRENT ASSETS Assets that are most easily converted to cash: cash equivalents such as certificates of deposit and U.S. Treasury bills, receivables, and inventory. Under generally accepted accounting principles, current assets are those that can be converted into cash within one year.

CURRENT LIABILITIES Liabilities that must be paid in one year or less; these typically include short-term loans, salaries, income taxes, and accounts payable.

CURRENT RATIO Current assets divided by current liabilities. This ratio is often used as a measure of a company's ability to meet currently maturing obligations.

DEBT RATIO The ratio of debt to either assets or equity in a company's financial structure.

DEPRECIATION A noncash expense that effectively reduces the balance-sheet value of an asset over its presumed useful life.

DISCOUNTED CASH FLOW (DCF) A method based on time-value-of-money concepts that calculate value by finding the present value of a business's future cash flows.

DUE DILIGENCE With respect to a public offering of securities, the investigation of facts and statements of risk made in the issuer's registration statement.

EBIT Earnings before interest and taxes.

EMPLOYEE STOCK OWNERSHIP PLAN (ESOP) In the United States, a formal plan under which corporate shares are acquired by the plan on behalf of employees, for whom it is a tax-qualified retirement plan.

ENTERPRISE VALUE The value of a company's equity plus its debt.

EQUITY BOOK VALUE The value of total assets less total liabilities.

EQUITY CAPITAL Capital contributed to a business that provides rights of ownership in return.

EXECUTIVE SUMMARY In a business plan, a short section that compellingly explains the opportunity, shows why it is timely, describes how the company plans to pursue it, outlines the entrepreneur's expectation of results, and includes a thumbnail sketch of the company and the management team.

FINANCIAL LEVERAGE See *leverage*.

FIXED ASSETS Assets that are difficult to convert to cash—for example, buildings and equipment. Sometimes called plant assets.

FIXED COSTS Costs incurred by the business that stay about the same no matter how many goods or services are produced.

GOOD FIT A situation in which the entrepreneur and management team have the managerial, financial, and technical capabilities and personal commitment needed to address a business opportunity.

GOODWILL An intangible balance-sheet asset. If a company has purchased another company for a price in excess of the fair market value of its assets, that "goodwill" is recorded as an asset. Goodwill may also represents intangible things such as the acquired company's excellent reputation, its brand names, or its patents, all of which may have real value.

GROSS PROFIT Sales revenues less the cost of goods sold. The roughest measure of profitability. Also called gross margin.

INCOME STATEMENT A financial statement that indicates the cumulative results of operations over a specified period. Also referred to as the profit-and-loss statement, or P&L.

INITIAL PUBLIC OFFERING (IPO) A corporation's first offering of its shares to the public.

INVENTORY The supplies, raw materials, components, and so forth that a company uses in its operations. It also includes work in process—goods in various stages of production—as well as finished goods waiting to be sold or shipped.

IPO See *initial public offering*.

LEVERAGE The degree to which the activities of a company are supported by liabilities and long-term debt as opposed to owners' capital contributions.

LIABILITY A claim against a company's assets.

LIFESTYLE ENTERPRISE   A business whose goal is to provide income and a retirement nest egg for the founder and his or her family.

LIMITED PARTNERSHIP   A hybrid form of organization having both limited and general partners. The general partner (there may be more than one) assumes management responsibility and unlimited liability for the business and must have at least a 1 percent interest in profits and losses. The limited partner (or partners) has no voice in management and is legally liable only for the amount of his or her capital contribution plus any other debt obligations specifically accepted.

MONEY MARKET   The network of issuers and dealers through which large borrowers raise short-term money by selling their debt instruments. This network represents both new issues and secondary market trading.

NET INCOME   The "bottom line" of the income statement. Net income is revenues less expenses less taxes. Also referred to as net earnings or net profits.

NET WORKING CAPITAL   Current assets less current liabilities; the amount of money a company has tied up in short-term operating activities.

OPERATING EARNINGS   On the income statement, gross margin less operating expenses and depreciation. Often called earnings before interest and taxes, or EBIT.

OPERATING EXPENSE   On the balance sheet, a category that includes administrative expenses, employee salaries, rents, sales and marketing costs, as well as other costs of business not directly attributed to the cost of manufacturing a product.

OPERATING LEVERAGE   The extent to which a company's operating costs are fixed versus variable. For example, a company that relies heavily on machinery and very few workers to produce its goods has a high operating leverage.

OWNERS' EQUITY   What, if anything, is left over after total liabilities are deducted from total assets. Owners' equity is the sum of capital contributed by owners plus their retained earnings. Also known as shareholders' equity.

PARTNERSHIP   A business entity with two or more owners. In the United States it is treated as a proprietorship for tax and liability purposes. Earnings are distributed according to the partnership agreement and are treated as personal income for tax purposes. Thus, like the sole proprietorship, the partnership is simply a conduit for generating income for its partners.

PREFERRED STOCK   An equity-like security that pays a specified dividend and has a superior position to common stock in case of distributions or liquidation.

PRESENT VALUE (PV)   The monetary value today of a future payment discounted at some annual compound interest rate.

PRICE-EARNINGS MULTIPLE   The price of a share of stock divided by earnings per share.

PRIVATE PLACEMENT   The sale of company stock to one or a few private investors instead of to the general public.

PROFIT-AND-LOSS STATEMENT (P&L)   See *income statement*.

PROFIT MARGIN   The percentage of every dollar of sales that makes it to the bottom line. Profit margin is net income after tax divided by net sales. Sometimes called the return on sales, or ROS.

PRO FORMA FINANCIAL STATEMENT   Financial statement (balance sheet or income statement) containing hypothetical or forecast data.

PROSPECTUS   A formal document that provides full disclosure to potential investors about the company, its business, its finances, and the way it intends to use the proceeds of its securities issuance. In its preliminary form it is known as a red herring.

REPLACEMENT VALUE   A valuation approach that estimates the cost of reproducing an asset, rather than the more common reliance on an asset's book value.

RETAINED EARNINGS   Annual net profits left after payment of dividends that accumulate on a company's balance sheet.

REVENUE   The amount of money that results from selling products or services to customers.

ROAD SHOW   A series of meetings between company officials and prospective investors, usually held in major cities around the country in conjunction with a forthcoming issue of corporate securities. The investors can put questions to the CEO or CFO about the company and the intended offering of securities.

S CORPORATION   In the United States, a closely held corporation whose tax status is the same as the partnership's but whose participants enjoy the liability protections granted to corporate shareholders. In other words, it is a conduit for passing profits and losses directly to the personal income tax returns of its shareholders, whose legal liabilities are limited to the amount of their capital contributions.

SOLE PROPRIETORSHIP   A business owned by a single individual. In the United States, this owner and the business are one and the same for tax and legal liability purposes. The proprietorship is not taxed as a separate entity. Instead, the owner reports all income and deductible expenses for the business on Schedule C of his or her personal income tax return.

SOLVENCY   The ability to pay bills as they come due.

STATEMENT OF FINANCIAL POSITION   See *balance sheet*.

STRATEGY   A plan that will differentiate the enterprise and give it a competitive advantage.

TIMES INTEREST EARNED RATIO   Earnings before interest and taxes divided by interest expense. Creditors use this ratio to gauge a company's ability to make future interest payments in the face of fluctuating operating results.

VARIABLE COSTS   Costs that rise or fall with the volume of output.

VENTURE CAPITALIST (VC)   A high-risk investor who seeks an equity position in a start-up or an early-growth company having high potential. In return for capital, the VC typically takes a significant percentage ownership of the business and a position on its board.

WARRANT   A security that gives the holder the right to purchase common shares of the warrant-issuing company at a stated price for a stated period of time. The stated price is generally set higher than the current valuation of the shares.

WORKING CAPITAL   See *net working capital*.

For Further Reading

Books

Bhidé, Amar, *The Origin and Evolution of New Businesses.* New York: Oxford University Press, 1999.

Who wants to be an entrepreneur? According to the author of this meticulously researched volume, "entrepreneurs who start and build new businesses are more celebrated than studied." Bhidé, an HBS Professor currently on leave to Columbia University, sets out to remedy the situation. By sharing the results of his decade-long research on hundreds of successful new businesses, tied in with classic theory, his book enlightens and informs readers—be they entrepreneurs, scholars, or even executives at large corporations—who'd like to inject a little entrepreneurial spirit into their projects. Bhidé's work demystifies the traits people normally ascribe to entrepreneurs so as to demonstrate precisely how a combination of luck, shrewd business skills, guts, and intelligence can launch a successful venture—or not.

Blowers, Stephen, Peter Griffith, and Tomas Milan. *The Ernst & Young Guide to the IPO Value Journey.* New York: John Wiley & Sons, 1999.

This handy book explains the entire journey to becoming a public company, beginning with an evaluation of the pros and cons of going public. It reviews the various levels of pre-IPO financing, estate tax issues for the entrepreneur, and all the steps you must take toward the event. Appendixes cover the details of writing a business plan, selecting the right stock market, resale restrictions, and an overview of U.S. Securities and Exchange Commission rules and regulations. Written for a U.S. audience.

Flamholtz, Eric, and Yvonne Randle, *Growing Pains: Transitioning from an Entrepreneurship to a Professionally Managed Firm.* San Francisco: Jossey-Bass, 2000.

Many entrepreneurial firms begin brilliantly, experience encouraging growth, but eventually fail. Others, in contrast, keep growing and growing, eventually taking their place among the ranks of mature and established enterprises. How can start-up companies master the challenge of rapid growth? Authors Flamholtz and Randle believe that many entrepreneurs are unprepared for the personal and organizational changes that growth requires. In their view, the loose, informal management styles that accounted for the entrepreneurs' initial success do not sustain them as they expand operations and staff up. The authors go on to describe seven stages of organizational growth and explain what must be accomplished in each stage to ensure continued success.

Gompers, Paul, and Josh Lerner. *The Money of Invention*. Boston: Harvard Business School Press, 2001.

Contrary to popular belief, the venture capital revolution is far from over. In fact, claim authors Paul Gompers and Josh Lerner, venture capital will continue to dramatically alter the American economic landscape. In this book they provide a definitive analysis of this powerful and unique industry and offer a meaningful framework for understanding the relationship between venture capital and entrepreneurial success. The authors offer actionable advice for managers of venture organizations, for entrepreneurs, and for all managers who seek returns from innovation in an environment that disdains hype and rewards careful, original thought and dogged execution. Readers will understand precisely how venture capital drives innovation, economic growth, and job creation.

Roberts, Edward B. *Entrepreneurship in High Technology: Lessons from MIT and Beyond*. New York: Oxford University Press, 1991.

The focus of this interesting book is on the formation and development of high-tech companies spawned by the scientific and military labs at MIT. Although much water has flowed over the dam in the years since the book was published, it nevertheless provides useful insights from a highly experienced scholar and practitioner who has worked for decades in one of America's hotbeds of high-tech entrepreneurship. Of particular interest are the chapters on the personal backgrounds of entrepreneurs.

Sahlman, William, Howard Stevenson, Michael Roberts, and Amar Bhidé, editors. *The Entrepreneurial Venture,* 2nd edition. Boston: Harvard Business School Press, 1999.

This well-chosen collection of articles by leading academics and practitioners covers basic entrepreneurial concepts and emerging issues. The text covers every phase of the entrepreneurial start-up, from evaluating opportunities to harvest. Profiles and examples from a variety of companies and fields illustrate the diverse, imaginative ways in which entrepreneurs think and act.

Siegal, Eric, Loren Schultz, Brian Ford, and David Carney. *The Ernst & Young Business Plan Guide*. New York: John Wiley & Sons, 1987.

This highly readable little book provides plenty of advice on how to write and develop business plans. Its worthwhile features include a realistic sample plan, guidelines for formatting and design, and tips on tailoring plans to particular decision makers.

Van Osnabrugge, Mark, and Robert J. Robinson. *Angel Investing: Matching Startup Funds with Startup Companies—A Guide for Entrepreneurs, Individual Investors, and Venture Capitalists.* San Francisco: Jossey-Bass, 2000.

Entrepreneurs who are eager to hook up with venture capital firms may be overlooking a more promising source of equity capital. According to these authors, business angels provide thirty to forty times as much financing to entrepreneurial firms each year as do venture capitalists, who get all the headlines. In this research-based book, Van Osnabrugge and Robinson tell readers where they can find these financiers and how they operate. Per their findings, the United States has almost three million angels, and their investments in start-up businesses is more than $60 billion per year.

Notes and Articles

Sahlman, William A. "How to Write a Great Business Plan." *Harvard Business Review,* July–August 1997.

This classic article by a seasoned scholar with deep experience in new ventures describes what financiers look for in a business plan and explores the mistakes entrepreneurs make in writing them. Most plans waste too much ink on numbers, according to Sahlman, and devote too little space to the information that truly matters to experienced investors: the people who will run the venture, the opportunity and its economic underpinnings, the context of the venture, and the risk/reward situation. If you have time to read only one short piece on business plan writing, read this article.

Wasserman, Noam. "Venture Capital Negotiations: VC versus Entrepreneur." Class Note 9-800-170. Boston: Harvard Business School Publishing, revised 2 March 2000.

The entrepreneur has the ideas, and the venture capitalist has the money. The entrepreneur wants to maintain control of his or her company and build it in line with a long-term vision. The VC wants to get in and get out quickly with a huge profit. Given these differences, it's not surprising that negotiations between these parties can be difficult. There is a great deal at stake, especially for the entrepreneur. This Harvard Business School case note describes the interests and goals of these two parties and explains how negotiations can be more productive.

Index

About the Subject Adviser

ALFRED E. OSBORNE JR., Ph.D., is Senior Associate Dean of the UCLA Anderson Graduate School of Management and director of the highly acclaimed Harold Price Center for Entrepreneurial Studies. The Price Center serves to organize all faculty research, student activities, and curricula related to the study of entrepreneurship and new-business development at UCLA Anderson. Dr. Osborne is an adviser and director to several public and private companies and is a frequent speaker and lecturer on entrepreneurial and corporate governance issues. He was an Economic Policy Fellow at the Brookings Institution and financial economist at the Securities and Exchange Commission, where his studies on capital market access and the liquidity of early investors brought changes to Rule 144 and the regulations affecting small and growing companies. Professor Osborne serves on the editorial board of the *International Journal of Entrepreneurship Education,* and he remains active in the entrepreneurial and venture development community and consults with small and growing companies on business and economic matters. He is a recipient of the Ernst & Young Entrepreneur of the Year award, the Richard J. Riordan Spirit of Entrepreneurship Award, and the BridgeGate 20 Award for his support of entrepreneurship in Southern California.

About the Writer

RICHARD LUECKE is the writer of several other books in the Harvard Business Essentials series. Based in Salem, Massachusetts, Mr. Luecke has authored or developed more than thirty books and dozens of articles on a wide range of business subjects. He has an M.B.A. from the University of St. Thomas.

Harvard Business Review Paperback Series

The Harvard Business Review Paperback Series offers the best thinking on cutting-edge management ideas from the world's leading thinkers, researchers, and managers. Designed for leaders who believe in the power of ideas to change business, these books will be useful to managers at all levels of experience, but especially senior executives and general managers. In addition, this series is widely used in training and executive development programs.

Books are priced at $19.95 U.S.
Price subject to change.

Title	Product #
Harvard Business Review **Interviews with CEOs**	3294
Harvard Business Review on **Advances in Strategy**	8032
Harvard Business Review on **Becoming a High Performance Manager**	1296
Harvard Business Review on **Brand Management**	1445
Harvard Business Review on **Breakthrough Leadership**	8059
Harvard Business Review on **Breakthrough Thinking**	181X
Harvard Business Review on **Building Personal and Organizational Resilience**	2721
Harvard Business Review on **Business and the Environment**	2336
Harvard Business Review on **Change**	8842
Harvard Business Review on **Compensation**	701X
Harvard Business Review on **Corporate Ethics**	273X
Harvard Business Review on **Corporate Governance**	2379
Harvard Business Review on **Corporate Responsibility**	2748
Harvard Business Review on **Corporate Strategy**	1429
Harvard Business Review on **Crisis Management**	2352
Harvard Business Review on **Culture and Change**	8369
Harvard Business Review on **Customer Relationship Management**	6994
Harvard Business Review on **Decision Making**	5572
Harvard Business Review on **Effective Communication**	1437

To order, call 1-800-668-6780, or go online at www.HBSPress.org

Title	Product #
Harvard Business Review on **Entrepreneurship**	9105
Harvard Business Review on **Finding and Keeping the Best People**	5564
Harvard Business Review on **Innovation**	6145
Harvard Business Review on **Knowledge Management**	8818
Harvard Business Review on **Leadership**	8834
Harvard Business Review on **Leadership at the Top**	2756
Harvard Business Review on **Leading in Turbulent Times**	1806
Harvard Business Review on **Managing Diversity**	7001
Harvard Business Review on **Managing High-Tech Industries**	1828
Harvard Business Review on **Managing People**	9075
Harvard Business Review on **Managing the Value Chain**	2344
Harvard Business Review on **Managing Uncertainty**	9083
Harvard Business Review on **Managing Your Career**	1318
Harvard Business Review on **Marketing**	8040
Harvard Business Review on **Measuring Corporate Performance**	8826
Harvard Business Review on **Mergers and Acquisitions**	5556
Harvard Business Review on **Motivating People**	1326
Harvard Business Review on **Negotiation**	2360
Harvard Business Review on **Nonprofits**	9091
Harvard Business Review on **Organizational Learning**	6153
Harvard Business Review on **Strategic Alliances**	1334
Harvard Business Review on **Strategies for Growth**	8850
Harvard Business Review on **The Business Value of IT**	9121
Harvard Business Review on **The Innovative Enterprise**	130X
Harvard Business Review on **Turnarounds**	6366
Harvard Business Review on **What Makes a Leader**	6374
Harvard Business Review on **Work and Life Balance**	3286

Management Dilemmas:
Case Studies from the Pages of
Harvard Business Review

How often do you wish you could turn to a panel of experts to guide you through tough management situations? The Management Dilemmas series provides just that. Drawn from the pages of *Harvard Business Review*, each insightful volume poses several perplexing predicaments and shares the problem-solving wisdom of leading experts. Engagingly written, these solutions-oriented collections help managers make sound judgment calls when addressing everyday management dilemmas.

These books are priced at $19.95 U.S.
Price subject to change.

Harvard Business Essentials

In the fast-paced world of business today, everyone needs a personal resource—a place to go for advice, coaching, background information, or answers. The Harvard Business Essentials series fits the bill. Concise and straightforward, these books provide highly practical advice for readers at all levels of experience. Whether you are a new manager interested in expanding your skills or an experienced executive looking to stay on top, these solution-oriented books give you the reliable tips and tools you need to improve your performance and get the job done. Harvard Business Essentials titles will quickly become your constant companions and trusted guides.

These books are priced at $19.95 U.S., except as noted.
Price subject to change.

Title	Product #
Harvard Business Essentials: **Negotiation**	1113
Harvard Business Essentials: **Managing Creativity and Innovation**	1121
Harvard Business Essentials: **Managing Change and Transition**	8741
Harvard Business Essentials: **Hiring and Keeping the Best People**	875X
Harvard Business Essentials: **Finance for Managers**	8768
Harvard Business Essentials: **Business Communication**	113X
Harvard Business Essentials: **Manager's Toolkit ($24.95)**	2896
Harvard Business Essentials: **Managing Projects Large and Small**	3213
Harvard Business Essentials: **Creating Teams with an Edge**	290X
Harvard Business Essentials: **Entrepreneur's Toolkit**	4368
Harvard Business Essentials: **Coaching and Mentoring**	435X
Harvard Business Essentials: **Crisis Management**	4376

The Results-Driven Manager

The Results-Driven Manager series collects timely articles from Harvard Management Update and Harvard Management Communication Letter to help senior to middle managers sharpen their skills, increase their effectiveness, and gain a competitive edge. Presented in a concise, accessible format to save managers valuable time, these books offer authoritative insights and techniques for improving job performance and achieving immediate results.

These books are priced at $14.95 U.S.
Price subject to change.

Readers of the Harvard Business Essentials series find the following Harvard Business School Press books of interest.

If you find these books useful:	You may also like these:
Negotiation (1113)	HBR on Negotiation and Conflict Resolution (2360) RDM Winning Negotiations That Preserve Relationships (3485)
Managing Creativity and Innovation (1121)	Creativity, Inc. (2077) Code Name Ginger (6730)
Managing Change and Transition (8741)	Leading Change (7471) The First 90 Days (1105)
Hiring and Keeping the Best People (875X)	The War for Talent (4592)
Business Communication (113X)	Working the Room (8199)
Manager's Toolkit ($24.95) (2896)	Smart Choices (8575) The Balanced Scorecard (6513)
Creating Teams with an Edge (290X)	The Wisdom of Teams (3670) Leading Teams (3332)
Entrepreneur's Toolkit (4368)	The Entrepreneurial Mindset (8346)
Coaching and Mentoring (435X)	Results-Based Leadership (8710) The Art of Possibility (7706)

How to Order

Harvard Business School Press publications are available worldwide from your local bookseller or online retailer.
You can also call

1-800-668-6780

Our product consultants are available to help you
8:00 a.m.–6:00 p.m., Monday–Friday, Eastern Time.
Outside the U.S. and Canada, call: 617-783-7450
Please call about special discounts for quantities greater than ten.

You can order online at

www.HBSPress.org

Need smart, actionable management advice?

Look no further than your desktop.

Harvard ManageMentor®, a popular online performance support tool from Harvard Business School Publishing, brings how-to guidance and advice to your desktop, ready when you need it, on a host of issues critical to your work. Now available in a PLUS version with audio-enhanced practice exercises.

Heading up a team? Resolving a conflict between employees? Preparing a make-or-break presentation for a client? Setting next year's budget? Harvard ManageMentor delivers practical advice, tips, and tools on over 30 topics right to your desktop—any time, just in time, and just in case you need it. Each topic includes:

1. Core Concepts: essential information in an easy-to-read format

2. Practical tips, tools, checklists, and planning worksheets

3. Interactive practice exercises and audio examples to enhance your learning

Try out two complimentary topics for Harvard ManageMentor® PLUS
by going to: **http://eLearning.harvardbusinessonline.org**

Harvard ManageMentor is available as a full online program with over 30 topics for $195 or as individual downloadable topics for $19.95 each. Selected topics are also available as printed Harvard ManageMentor Business Guides for $12.95 each and on CD-ROM (4 topics each) for only $49.95. For site license and volume discount pricing call 800.795.5200 (outside the U.S. and Canada: 617.783.7888) or visit http://eLearning.harvardbusinessonline.org.